More than a Religion

– A Relationship

by Craig Emerson Strain

ISBN 9781706251217

More than a Religion – A Relationship

According to the Bible. Faith is a substance.

Hebrews 11:1 *"Now faith is the substance of things hoped for, the evidence of things not seen."*

It is a real substance that you can see, know, understand, and work with.

But faith without works is dead. You have got to put the "I" in faith. In my years of being a "born again Christian", the Lord has blessed me to follow him in a wonderful way. This book covers some things that I have done, that you always wished you could do, but didn't. But you can learn what I learned because I did it. There have been several books that I have read in my life that "stirred" up my faith in believing what God can do. I want to give you a book with what I have seen that has stirred up my faith.

I dedicate this book to my cousin Larry Strain. He has encouraged me multiple times to sit down and write the wonderful things God has done and remind us what God can and will do with us and for us.

Larry overcame paralysis from a minor outpatient surgery mistake. It took months of therapy for him to begin to move his legs, and years of therapy to begin to walk, and years of persevering to get to the place that he could lead a full life. Three years from being paralyzed, back to walking and being productive again. Faith is substance.

Multiple times Larry encouraged me to take the time and effort to put some thoughts on paper. Thanks, Larry. Learning to walk again would be harder to do.

I dedicate this book also to Bro Arles Smith, a constant encouragement. "When are you going to write a book?" Well, Bro Arles, here it is!

Last, but not least, I dedicate this book to my wife Linda Strain. To all the late nights and early mornings, she saw me toiling over the computer, pecking away at the keyboard. Thanks, Linda.

Thank you, Waldo Emerson Wood. Your name lives on.

Forethought

I was looking at the ceiling again. Popcorn ceiling, they call it. People pay money on all the DIY shows on TV to get rid of it. I don't know why they don't like it. But when I was a kindergartener, bedfast, suffering with Rheumatic Fever, it is the most exciting ceiling that you could have. It had infinite possibilities for exploration for a child whose body was weak, and his mind was active.

I had a base camp straight up from the bed. From there I would explore down the canyon on the "moonscape" that was above me. I wouldn't cheat and cross over the mountain range that was made up with the popcorn, I had to stay disciplined and follow the canyon and valleys to work my way around to the backside of the mountain range. I should be able to get there before lunch and back to the base camp before my sister, Colleen, gets back from school.

Thus, began my memories of childhood. But every once in a while, on a trip in my own world, on my own ceiling, a comforting "Presence" would come into the room and fill it with warmth and peace. I knew then that I was OK. Who or what was that "Presence" that would slip into the room? I always wondered.

I don't know how sick I was, but I remember when spring came, dad put the training wheels on my bicycle. It was so great to be on my bike. I remember seeing my sister crying as I tried my best to pedal the bicycle forward.

Contents

Forethought

I was looking at the ceiling again. Popcorn ceiling, they call it. People pay money on all the DIY shows on TV to get rid of it. I don't know why they don't like it. But when I was a kindergartener, bedfast, suffering with Rheumatic Fever, it is the most exciting ceiling that you could have. It had infinite possibilities for exploration for a child whose body was weak, and his mind was active.

I had a base camp straight up from the bed. From there I would explore down the canyon on the "moonscape" that was above me. I wouldn't cheat and cross over the mountain range that was made up with the popcorn, I had to stay disciplined and follow the canyon and valleys to work my way around to the backside of the mountain range. I should be able to get there before lunch and back to the base camp before my sister, Colleen, gets back from school.

Thus, began my memories of childhood. But every once in a while, on a trip in my own world, on my own ceiling, a comforting "Presence" would come into the room and fill it with warmth and peace. I knew then that I was OK. Who or what was that "Presence" that would slip into the room? I always wondered.

I don't know how sick I was, but I remember when spring came, dad put the training wheels on my bicycle. It was so great to be on my bike. I remember seeing my sister crying as I tried my best to pedal the bicycle forward.

Contents

Chapter 1   Things which we have seen and heard.

Acts 4:20 *"For we cannot but speak the things which we have seen and heard."*

To start a walk with the Lord, you must make sure that what you do is according to the Bible.   I will quote many versus that go along with my thoughts.

My first step was realizing what a mess of my life I had let it become.   Having dropped out of college, I was looking for work. College for me was great.   I had been to a lot of places, met a lot of people, and learned a lot of things.   I attended so many activities my first year in school, I didn't realize that I needed to devote more time to getting good grades and establishing a good grade point average. I was a member of the University Choir, Men's Glee Club, orchestra and Marching Band along with hours in the music labs.

I was there, both feet in.   I loved music, so I studied to be a music teacher, hopefully to be a band director.   My love of music during the '70's of course was Big Band music, Classical Music, Marching Music, and Rock Music.   None of these gave me direction in life but opened many doors to participate in activities that not everyone would have a chance at.   While I was at Ball State University, I was a part of the University Marching Band.   The discipline was fantastic, 250 people trying for a goal of being at the right place, at the right time, and being in perfect alignment.   I so enjoyed that level of perfection that Band music inspired.

Our band was voted number #1 College Marching Band in the nation according to CBS and we were chosen to march at the NFL Championship game in 1967.   Dallas Cowboys with Coach Tom Landry verses the Green Bay Packers with legendary Coach Vince Lombardy. Two of the greatest NFL teams with the two historic coaches of all time. What we didn't realize, at the time, was this football game, held in Wisconsin, was also going to be the coldest NFL game in history. It became known as the "Ice Bowl" at -14 true

1

temperature and at -54 degrees wind chill at game time. It was Cold! To this day, ESPN, Weather Channel and all records refers to this historic game.

I was in the percussion section and it was so cold that we taped the drumsticks to our hands because we couldn't tell if we were holding any sticks in our hands.

It was so cold that the trumpets, tubas, trombones and all brass instruments; they took fingernail polish and coated the mouthpieces so their lips wouldn't stick to the mouthpiece.

It was so cold that the brass players used kerosene and vodka in the valves and slides so the oil wouldn't get thick and freeze up.

It was so cold that the Referee's whistle froze to his mouth, so he just left it in until it froze to his lips.

It was so cold that the pea froze in the whistle.

It was so cold!

As the game was coming to the final minutes, the band went in behind in the end zone to get ready to perform "post-game" and march onto the frozen field. *We were so cold.*

The Packers lined up and broke through the line for the final winning touchdown with seconds to go. The ball carrier ran right through the band. *We were so cold.*

But something happens. In your numbness of the freezing temperature, as this huge football player runs past you, you realize that you are on TV! It hits you first in the lower back, moves up the spine, makes you throw out your arms, and you look up to where the cameras are and yell "HEY, MOM!"

And sure enough, you scream and go crazy thinking that Mom sees you and is proud. "That's my boy." Really? Suddenly you just did what you've seen countless others do and you always wondered, "Why do they always do that?"

I enjoyed going to many places where rock bands played. I remember a little room on campus called "The Loft" that we would go to on weekends at Ball State. One night there was only 15 - 20 people in the crowd, and the band only had 3 people in it. So we started to leave, but then the band started playing. They were so good, whoever this band was, they were going to change music as we know it. The guitar player was a guy named, Jimi Hendrix.

At another place that we would go, called Indiana Beach, I had a date with a sorority girl. The band was playing, and we were all out there just dancing away, when a girl singer got up on the platform. She started to really sing. I asked my date if we could just stop and listen. We went up to the platform right at the singer's feet. She was good. Everyone in the place (200 – 300 people) eventually stopped and listened. The group was called "Big Brother and the Holding Company" and they were trying out a singer named "Janis Joplin".

At the end of that year, I transferred to a Community College in central Florida, hoping to get my grades back up to where they should be, but my "party attitude" kind of put me in the center of the school spotlight. I moved in with an old friend from Indiana who suggested this school. Now I was 1,100 miles from home and only knew one person on campus. It was really lonely. When I would be changing from one class to another, I would be watching for that only person that I knew. Well, I lost my contact lenses and I couldn't see any faces. I would say "Hi" to someone that I thought I knew, and sure enough, I didn't know them, but I would go ahead and strike up a conversation with them. It really was lonely talking to all these strangers.

Little did I know or understand that the Bible is true even if you don't read it, study it, or believe it. Because I spend the first year talking to people I didn't even know, by the end of the year, I was elected to be a "Campus Favorite" in the School Yearbook. It was so strange to be so popular and yet so alone.

Proverbs 18:24   *A man that hath friends must shew himself friendly; and there is a friend that sticketh closer than a brother.*

I was then elected to be the student director of the Student Activities Committee. Being the student director of the committee, I oversaw all the activities and programs that the college brought in. Whatever was going to happen required the combined vote of the Student Counsel (of which were by now all friends of mine), the President of the College, and the Director of the Student Activities (my committee).

We always had a "sock hop" to start the year off with, but I thought that was too old fashioned. Woodstock had been and I knew things were different now. So I changed the format and brought a group in for a concert. Since I spearheaded the idea, the college let me pick the group. I picked a group called "The First Addition." Nobody had ever heard of them, so, many people didn't know what to expect, but the band had a singer with them that they were trying out. His name was Kenny Rogers. Well the rest was history.

The time period for youth in America was difficult. Drugs where a big part of the Rock Music scene. Rock Concerts with the big named groups involved free use of drugs being passed around during the concerts. I saw groups like The Who, Jefferson Airplane, Rod Stewart, Humble Pie, Black Sabbath, Almond Brothers and the list goes on and on. Central Florida had a constant flow of drugs going through it. The most "pot" that I personally saw was 17 large hefty trash bags coming off an airplane. One of these bags went to someone that I personally knew.

I had moved into an apartment complex off campus and little by little brought in foreign exchange students and took over the complex. I enjoyed helping them get acclimated to the US and I enjoyed learning about their culture. Edgar Lopez from Columbia, Mohammed from Pakistan, Helmut from Germany, each of these people let me learn much about their culture and religions.

Easter came and my roommate at the time was Brad. We took the weekend to go to Daytona Beach for spring break with a bunch of our friends. Spring break at Daytona was a huge college event. We smoked a lot of "pot", drank a lot of alcohol and did a lot of body surfing in the ocean. When it came time to leave, Brad decided to ride back with some other friends. When I got back home, there was a note on the door with a phone number to call. When I called, they told me that, "Brad was killed in a car wreck, but not to worry, Brad didn't suffer. He had just enough time to curse God as he went thru the windshield."

I knew I had to make a change in my life and lifestyle.

I decided to drop out of school and try to get my life started again. So strange, I had no job, no degree, nobody to turn to for a job. I moved in with my mom, who had now moved down to Florida, and I went hunting for a job.

I called companies, knocked on doors, searched the want ad papers, did everything that you do to get a job. Nothing worked. In fact, one company that I went to just to get a job washing cars, they asked me to not come back and not bother them. I had been visiting all these companies each week asking for a job.

It was during this time that I remembered when I used to sing in the choir in our Methodist Church back in my hometown. I remembered the direction, or hope for tomorrow, or purpose that life seemed to have back then. I decided to go back to Church. Well, not like before, because I was much different now. As I walked up to the big Methodist Church in Winter Park Florida, I finished off a huge marijuana joint. In fact, I held my breath as I walked in the Church so I could have the full effects of the "rush" for Church.

The pipe organ exploded in this fantastic music and the choir was so cool. But when the Minister asked the Church to bow their heads in prayer, this little old lady next to me began to "talk to Him". I was never so touched in all my life! She knew Him! She was talking to God! This little old lady let me know that He did exist and that He

5

could be a friend. Immediately I knew that if He could love her, maybe He could love me!

As I sat there, I now knew that I had to find Him. The offering plate came by and I reached in my pocket, just like I always did as a child, and put in a quarter. I was so embarrassed. God was now watching, and I put money in as a little kid. Right then and there I thought in my heart. "God, get me a job and I will pay my tithes."

Proverbs 3:9 *Honour the LORD with thy substance, and with the first fruits of all thine increase:*

Chapter 2   Acknowledge Him

Proverbs 3:6 *In all thy ways acknowledge him, and he shall direct thy paths.*

Monday morning was still Monday morning, I still needed a job. But the difference was that now God and I had a secret. That morning the phone rang. The company on the other end wanted to know if I still wanted to wash cars. Weeks before, they asked me not to come back, but now they wanted to know if I was still interested to work for them. Of course, I said "YES" and at the same time, I realized that God heard my prayer and had opened up the door.

Revelation 3:8 *I know thy works: behold, I have set before thee an open door, and no man can shut it: for thou hast a little strength, and hast kept my word, and hast not denied my name.*

Starting this job was amazing. Here I was washing cars at Avis Rent A Car. Three years of college behind me, and I am washing cars for a living. But I really was thankful. I was working at McCoy AFB in Orlando. It was a growing area. I was working with a bunch of guys that were Viet Nam vets, so we worked hard and stayed "stoned" most of the day. I got my own apartment and was starting to get my life going again. I went back to the Methodist Church a couple of times, but I wasn't looking for Church, I was wondering about Him.

I had been at the Rental car company for about 6 months when they wanted to move me to the downtown office. It was closer to where I lived, the hours were better and I was having to do quite a bit more, when one morning the office called me in and wanted to know if I was willing to move to another position. I said yes and ended up as the assistant manager to the new Rental Car facility at Disney World! Way too cool! I was at Disney every day and we were beating our competitor "Hertz" by giving better service to our customers. Somehow the big wigs of Hertz in NYC heard about this 6'6" tall guy with a red Avis jacket renting cars at Disney World when they had paid $$$$ to be the Official Rental Car Company of Disney World.

They reassigned me back to the main office of washing cars and working the front desk. I was truly disappointed that I was being removed from the Disney location. It was on a Monday morning again when they called me in a big meeting. They thanked me for the good job out at Disney World but told me of a lawsuit that Hertz threatened to start so they had to move me out of sight. It wasn't sounding good, but they offered me another job. They couldn't tell me where, all they wanted to know was, did I want to take it?

I asked where and they said they couldn't tell me. I asked them "When do you want to know." They said, "right now".

What happened next was truly amazing. I had never heard of the "Holy Ghost". I did not know that you could feel "God" or know that "God" was in the plan, or however you want to word it. But the best I can say. This "presence" fell on me and I felt the greatest peace that anyone could feel about making a decision. I told them yes! They said, "Great" as the Regional manager open the desk drawer and handed me an airline ticket. He said, "Your plane leaves in the morning at 7:45 am and you will be moving to Panama City Beach to be the new Airport Manager for Avis-Rent-a-Car!" I didn't even know where Panama City was. I had to go look it up on the map to find it. It is known as a really wild place for College students during spring break.

By this time, I had acquired all the stuff that success is supposed to bring to a Yuppie. I now was on my 2nd Italian Fiat 124 Sport Coupe, a nice duplex on the Gulf of Mexico, and the manager of the Car Rental Company at the International Airport. I had a stereo system in my apartment that I could "blow out a burning match" with the volume turned up. I could take any car off the lot for my personal use, fly for free on the company expense account, fly free anywhere in the state of Florida on a certain airline and any airport that I landed at, I had a card that said that I was a V.I.P. and was given a rental car for free. I was the youngest Airport Manager in the AVIS Corporation.

I totally enjoyed the work, the hours, the responsibility, the benefits, and the trust of the company. I had a staff of four in the terminal and others in fleet support. My weekends were going from bar to bar and listening to the bands which were so good because of the huge tourist attractions.

When the rock concerts would come into the area, I would supply the bands and staff with rental cars, so they would invite me to the parties in the motels before the concerts with the band members. I had a "shag" haircut like Rod Stewart and a mustache with little wire frame glasses. Life was good!

Meanwhile, I met a fellow named Terry that carried luggage for Southern Airways, he would always take time to talk with me. We started eating lunch together and just became friends. One day he asked me a question that was a scripture.

Mark 8:36 *For what shall it profit a man, if he shall gain the whole world, and lose his own soul?*

No scripture could have come any closer to describing my life at that point. As my success in business was good, my personal life was getting worse. It was almost like I was selling my soul to gain the world. I would fly to Miami or Atlanta for training sessions during the day, and then go bar hopping in the evening to some of the "best" and worst joints till early in the morning.

But back at the airport, Terry would always take time with me and share his love of Jesus to me. He never pushed it on me. He was a friend that shared with me the best thing in his life. I finally asked him to "tone it down" a bit. I wanted to see if Jesus really wanted me. He laughed a "good natured" laugh and told me to "Watch what God will do".

It was amazing. One day one of the National Airline's scheduled flights came in. The pilot was taking his lunch break in the cafeteria, but instead, he walked over to my counter and said to me "The Lord is dealing with your heart!"

Another time, the CASE equipment company's private plane came in, the executives took off in the rental car and the private pilot came up to me and asked me if I was a Christian! I thought that I would quote a scripture to get this fellow to not "witness" to me. I told him,

Matthew 18:20 *For where two or three are gathered together in my name, there am I in the midst of them.*

Suddenly, the "Holy Ghost" came down on me again just like I felt back in Orlando when they asked me to take this assignment. I was amazed! I got out from behind the rental counter and quickly walked on down the concourse to the outside of the airport. I couldn't believe it! I looked behind me, and sure enough, here comes the pilot walking to catch up. He had this big grin on his face looking like a fisherman who had just hooked a big fish and was going to reel him in.

He asked me again if I was a Christian. I told him that I wasn't, but I had been searching. He smiled big and said to me, "You're getting really close!"

Do you know, if he had asked me to pray with him, I would have rejected his prayer, but when he showed me that he had confidence that God was doing a perfect work, that really encouraged me. I knew that, somehow, I was getting closer.

Chapter 3   **A way that seemeth right**

Living in a beach town with a lot of tourist made for an exciting life. There were plenty of bars and bands. But what made things different was I was a "local". You kind of looked at the tourists as "tourists" and those that were local you looked as "locals". It put you in a different light to those around you. I knew all the lifeguards, most of the waiters and waitresses in the restaurants and best of all, I knew most of the bands that played in the bars up and down the beach. But to me the best setup was that when the Rock Concerts came into our area, I supplied the cars to the staff and bands.

I had met some promoters when I put on the rock concert at the college, so this just opened the door to working with them when they came to Panama City Beach. Groups like Jefferson Airplane came, and I had met the leader of the group. He always liked a convertible so I would have one ready for him. I would always be invited to the concerts and would be invited to the hotel for the parties before and after the concerts.

Even though I wasn't a Christian, there was always something that I saw that made me question what was going on. A lot of the bands, even though they were famous and all that, they weren't really any better musicians than the average musicians. I played drums thru high school and college; a lot of these drummers weren't any better than myself. I had been in a rock band, back in High School, that played at all the school dances after the football and basketball games. I would have loved to be in a Rock band and be successful.

But their lifestyle was quite a bit different. There are things that I saw that really made me wonder. Some were into hard drugs, some were into alcohol, others were into the groupies that chased after the bands, others were into mystic religions and so forth. To me, it seemed that they had sold their soul to get where they were. I always fit in the music and marijuana group. You just kind of pick the crowd that you fit in with.

But one night, I was listening to an album that the local underground radio station was playing. It was a group playing a "live recording" of their songs. It was the best live album that I had ever heard. They were really good.

So this next day, the groups arrived at the airport, my staff fixed up the bands with cars while I talked with the promoters. That night I went to the Holiday Inn to be with the bands before the concert. I went into one room that seemed pretty lively. The music was turned up and the room was turned on. To say that the roomed was filled with smoke would be an understatement.

I met one person in the room, and we talked for a while and were discussing different albums that were out there. I mentioned that I heard one of the best "live" albums that I have ever heard. He looked kind of amazed at me and turned to get someone else in the room. He came back with someone and said to him. "Peter, he's heard our album and he said it was good."

This was the band that was on the album. The fellow was Peter Frampton who was the leader of the group named "Humble Pie". We all talked a while before Peter returned with the others. What happened next was what I call an "Aha" moment. It is one of those moments that you seem to see things clearly.

Here I was, a successful young businessperson who always wanted to be in a rock band, talking with a band member who was in a rock band, traveling the country and actually the world.

I now had a "shag" haircut, little wire framed glasses and a mustache. I had a great job, living in a great place, going to good concerts, smoking marijuana with the best of groups, and looking conservative enough to not be troubled by police. And here I stood before a band member that was traveling around the world, real long hair, smoking marijuana, and playing before large crowds of people.

It was at this time that we both really took a look at each other and we realized that we were both just playing a game. I looked like a straight guy and he was looking like a hippy guy, but we were both just playing roles. I, a successful businessman and him a famous musician. We both realized that neither one of us had the answer. We were playing roles, putting up an image of fulfillment and personal satisfaction that neither one of us had.

Proverbs 14:12 *There is a way which seemeth right unto a man, but the end thereof are the ways of death.*

When I left that night, I really wondered about the direction that I was going, where it would take me, and would my life ever have real meaning. No doubt, the fellow with the band would also consider his choices in life and where they were going to take him.

It was only a few days later that life turned so good for me. My hope was that this bass player had change in his life also for the good.

Chapter 4   "Would you pray for me?"

John 3:7 *Marvel not that I said unto thee, Ye must be born again.*

It was a Saturday. A beautiful day. Everything was caught up in the office. I was going to take a day off at the beach. Living on the beach was nice, especially on Panama City Beach. The sand was sugar white and at this time, very few people lived year-round in this area. Panama City Beach bragged on the phrase of being the best kept secret. My apartment was a brick duplex with no houses for a mile when I looked out my windows. The road along the beach was so desolate after Labor Day, that I would ride my bicycle 12 miles down the beach to where all the shops and motels were at. The road was so desolate that I would put my tire on the white line and never have to look up.

This day, the waves were bigger than usual. On any given day, the waves would only be one to two feet tall. But today they were three and four feet tall.

I enjoyed body surfing. Having been on the swimming team back in High School, I enjoyed water. The Red Cross would give a patch to every person that would swim 50 miles. I got the patch 3 times. Needless to say, I enjoyed swimming.

Body surfing was as close to the waves as you could get. You had to make a quick sprint at the right time to catch the speed of the wave. As you were picked up by the wave, you could then shape your body to turn left or right or speed up or slow down. You could do whatever you needed to do to keep in the wave.

This day the waves were larger than usual. Four feet doesn't sound like a big wave, but when you look up at a wave as you are swimming, that is four feet up from your chin to the crest of the wave. I had been in waves larger than that, but this was good enough for some fun.

I walked down to the beach and went out were a sandbar was making the waves break better. The water was warm, as it always was even in September, and the day was sunny. I rode waves all morning long and then took a break for lunch. I remember taking a shower when I got back home. I felt sandy and gritty from the salty water. It was so good that morning that I decided to go back again for the afternoon. A whole day of surfing. Life was good.

At about 3 o'clock, I had had enough and went home. I couldn't have asked for a better day. I took another shower to wash off the salt and the sand. I was enjoying my life, enjoying the day off, but I had this nagging feeling of just being "dirty". I had enjoyed a great day of surfing but still felt that I was still missing something great in my life. I went and ate some dinner and decided to go to the airport.

As I walked up to the concourse, I saw Terry at the ticket counter. Terry had been a friend that was patient and always willing to tell me about Jesus. Even when I asked him to not "push it" so much, Terry was always there. So, as I walked up to the counter, he said "Hi" and we started on some small talk, I just stopped the conversation and said, "Terry, would you pray for me?"

Terry was a good witness for the Lord. He never treated me like I was some "big shot" even though I was the manager of the Avis Rent-A-Car and he was basically a baggage handler for the airlines. He was a very honest and open fellow. And I knew I could ask him any question that I wanted and get a truthful answer. But the strange thing was that Terry would always ask me the questions and I would answer.

He would ask me a question like, "If you died, do you know where you would go?" So, I would start off with some answer that sounded like I understood everything about what I knew, and the more I spoke, the more I understood that I didn't know anything.

But his willingness to listen to me made me want to listen to what he had to say. I could see that he really knew what he was talking about. He didn't talk about God from a religious viewpoint, but he talked about Jesus from a relationship knowledge. He knew Him!

15

I remember one day at the airport when I saw someone treat Terry very badly. I knew that it had to hurt him. He had a family at home to feed and any tips from someone was always good. I believe that the airways changed his hours so that he was working some of the slower times of day. That would affect what his tips would bring. They had "done him wrong." So, I went up to him, I guess in a mischievous way just to see how he would react. He could have told me how bad they had treated him, but instead, he just let the situation not bother him. To me, his relationship with the "Lord" was real.

As Terry saw me walking up to the counter on this slow afternoon, Terry later told me that his thoughts were," Lord, I've told him everything I know about you. Please, just let him ask for prayer."

As I walked up to the counter, all the talk was just "filler and niceties," I needed something and I didn't know what it was, so I asked Terry, "Terry, would you pray for me?"

I sat down on the scales where your bags are weighed. Terry told me that I had sin in my life and that I would never be happy or fulfilled until I ask for forgiveness. He told me that the only way for forgiveness was to ask Jesus to forgive me. Jesus went to the cross and died for my sin. He said it was up to me to ask for forgiveness.

John 14:6 *Jesus saith unto him, I am the way, the truth, and the life: no man cometh unto the Father, but by me.*

It was all so simple, but it seemed so true. I had believed that God exists, but I never prayed to Jesus to be forgiven.

I began to pray and ask for forgiveness. Terry led me in a sinner's prayer, but my heart was more open than just my words. I really wanted something in my life. But as I prayed, something happened. Nobody had ever told me that you would feel the Lord come into your life. Nobody ever told me that you would feel your heart change. Nobody ever told me that you would feel the burdens of sin being lifted off your heart.

My hands began to sweat, and I could see dirt coming out of my pours.

The dirt that I felt in my soul, was coming out of my hands too. I said to Terry "Look at my hands, they are clean!" Terry probably thought that I was being a little dramatic, but I really felt the difference and change in my life! I was forgiven!

Thinking back to this time, I should have checked the scales that I was setting on to see if I was lighter now that the weight of sin was removed from my life.

Chapter 5   **A new creature:**

2nd Corinthians 5:17 *Therefore if any man be in Christ, he is a new creature: old things are passed away; behold, all things are become new.*

Monday morning at the office, my whole staff knew that something was different. They knew my lifestyle, they knew my disposition, they knew my moods, but now they all saw that everything was different! That first week just flew by, when the weekend came, I thought about how I usually spent the weekend, getting "stoned", bar hopping, listening to the bands. What do I do now? I knew that I didn't want that anymore.

So, I decided to spend the same amount of time praying that I would have spent getting "stoned". Now, mind you, I had plenty of my "stash" left in the house. But how do you pray when you know God is really listening? What do you say to a living God?

Do I ask for a new car? I had over 50 of them at my disposal plus my Italian Sports car. Do I ask for a new home? I had a nice one on the Gulf of Mexico. Do I ask for a new job? I was so pleased with the one he "gave" me.

So not knowing what to say, what to pray, how to pray, I just sat down in the middle of the floor and opened my Bible. I didn't even know where to begin reading, look how big the Bible is! So, where I randomly opened the Bible, the verse that I started reading at said:

1st Timothy 2:8 *I will therefore that men pray everywhere, lifting up holy hands, without wrath and doubting.*

How perfect could God's direction be, when he knew I doubted what to do and how to pray! So, I lifted up my hands and began to pray. Now mind you, I had never seen anyone pray. The only Church that I had been to and we only just bowed our head. I had never read about these scriptures.

I lifted up my hands like the Bible said and just began to thank God for what he had done in my life. It wasn't easy. It was a conflict. I prayed for only a few moments and I decided to get up.

I remember that I said to myself that I was going to spend the same time praying that I would have done spend getting "stoned". So, I sat back down again. I lifted up my hands and prayed some more. It still seemed like a lot of conflict. After praying a few moments more, I thought about getting up and getting a drink of water. So, as I started to get up. I realized that I wasn't even thirsty. My goodness, what a battle. When I have set in my heart to pray, so much did not want me to pray. I sat back down and began to pray once again.

This time my thoughts said, "people were going to make fun of you for praying". What a Lie! Here I was, in my room, nobody for a mile outside my window. What a lie!

I lifted up my hands again, with the sole purpose of praising God, and as I prayed out loud, I began to pray in another language. What a blessing! What was this? It just flowed out of my mouth, this heavenly language!

I had never heard of anything like this! It was wonderful! I hadn't lost my mind or anything. I had a very sound mind, but I stopped praying. I had done a lot of foolish things before. I really didn't want to go off on some religious tangent. I didn't want to chase after some strange religious thing only to find out that it wasn't right. So, I decided to stop praying and instead take this time to read the Bible. I knew it would be better to be scripturally correct than to be led off the wrong direction.

But once again, where do you start reading this Bible? So, I just opened the book to wherever it opened and just start reading. It was somewhere in the middle that I began to read, and it read like this.

Acts 2:1-4 *And when the day of Pentecost was fully come, they were all with one accord in one place.*

> *And suddenly there came a sound from heaven as of a rushing mighty wind, and it filled all the house where they were sitting.*
>
> *And there appeared unto them cloven tongues like as of fire, and it sat upon each of them.*
>
> *And they were all filled with the Holy Ghost, and began to **speak with other tongues**, as the Spirit gave them utterance.*
>
> .

Truly amazing! I was praying in tongues just like the Bible said! It was the Holy Ghost that was giving me the utterance. Praise God! I kept on reading that night because now the Bible was so understandable. It was as if the same inspiration that moved upon these guys to write these scriptures, was the same understanding that I now had. It just made perfect sense.

Monday morning came around, I got ready to shower and shave. I looked into the mirror and saw the eyes of a person that I had never seen before. Eyes that were clear, eyes that had depth. I was a new person!

Matthew 6:22 *The light of the body is the eye: if therefore thine eye be single, thy whole body shall be full of light.*

I saw Terry that morning at the airport and I told him what happened that weekend. I told him about my praying that night, and how the "Holy Ghost" just prayed through me. I told him how easy it was to pray and read and just feel the blessings of God. He kind of looked at me and said. "I've heard of that before. I had someone in a prayer meeting pray like that." I was kind of excited and told him that this was so good, and he should pray on and "get it" too.

Acts 2:39 *For the promise is unto you, and to your children, and to all that are afar off, even as many as the Lord our God shall call.*

John 7:38 *He that believeth on me, as the scripture hath said, out of his belly shall flow rivers of living water.*

Chapter 6   Are you missing anything?

A week or two later, I was at home reading from the Bible. As I was reading, it seemed like my left leg was missing. It wasn't asleep, it was as if it wasn't there anymore. I could see it, but it had no feeling in it as if it was missing. I thought about it, I was missing a leg, but I was still complete in God. If I had been missing an arm, I would still be whole in the Lord. What if I was missing an eye, or missing a mind? I realized that we are complete when we are made whole by Jesus.

As I continued reading, my leg began to feel normal again. It didn't get heavy as it would if it had fallen asleep. I just acknowledged that even though I was missing a part of me, I was still complete in Jesus.

The next morning, I was on the way to the airport. I had passed a nursing home each and every day without noticing it. But this morning, this nursing home seemed significant. So I pulled into the parking lot and went in. I didn't have a clue of the purpose of this stop. I didn't know a single soul that was in there or worked inside, so I just started down a hallway. As I came to the end, there was the sign that said "EXIT". I thought, "Lord, why did you send me to this dead end?" As I turned to go back, I looked in the last room, and there was a man lying in the bed with his left leg missing.

He said to me, "Come on in Preacher. The Lord told me you were coming."

Here was this elderly man in the nursing home. He looked at me and said, "God told me to tell you that you are a singer and a Preacher, don't you forget it!"

I have never forgotten what he told me. He went on to say, "The Lord put me in this nursing home. The Lord would wake me up and send me to someone's room. I'm the last person to pray with some of these people before they die." He showed me how he could swing himself into the wheelchair beside the bed. He'd then roll on down to whatever room he was sent into.

It was amazing. I guess the Lord let me "lose my leg" the night before so I wouldn't judge the man that wasn't "whole". But this fellow had a purpose that he knew that only he could fulfill. Some people would complain that nobody visits them, but here he was, visiting people.

Matthew 25:43 *I was a stranger, and ye took me not in: naked, and ye clothed me not: sick, and in prison, and ye visited me not.*

This fellow gave me an insight to how we should live our lives for God.

Chapter 7   The Lord Told Me

Proverbs 3:5 *Trust in the Lord with all thine heart; and lean not unto thine own understanding.*

I trusted the Lord to lead me and bless my business. The staff saw the change in my life, I shared with them that I had gotten saved and then the Lord gave me the "Holy Ghost" with the evidence of speaking in tongues! They showed a lot of respect to me and trusted in my decisions. I wanted to devote a few personal minutes when I went into the office each morning for prayer. We shared things that we wanted to pray about and not a morning began without prayer for God's blessings and guidance.

Besides being the Airport Manager with Avis Rent-A-Car, I was also the "Key Operator" for the North Florida district. I was flown to Miami and Atlanta for computer training classes. As the "Key Operator", I was the support person for the computer system that was being first tested and installed in our district. This very same system is now in use across the nation. They had a contest for someone to name the system and one of the gals from our district won with the name "Watson the Wizard", which the name is still used this day.

I knew the workings of the system well and made all my business plans from the readouts and reports. But one morning as I was taking my personal prayer time, I felt impressed of the Lord to get more cars into my airport. I looked at the manifests and reservation reports and saw no need for more cars. But I "knew" that the Lord was directing me to get more cars.

Proverbs 3:6 *In all thy ways acknowledge him, and he shall direct thy paths.*

I checked on the computer for the fleet status across the district and placed all available cars on hold for me to arrange transportation into my airport. I called drivers to shuttle cars in, I ordered tractor trailers to pick up cars and bring them to Panama City. I even called to airports in southern Alabama and Georgia, to send me their available cars. This was on a Friday. The Avis Business rule was to not bring in cars on a Friday because businesspeople would be checking in the cars that they had out during the week. You do not run up the expense for something that you will not need.

Well, the district manager heard that I was bringing in cars from across the district and out of state. Now this fellow and I had been "good friends" before I had become a Christian. We would go bar hopping, and drinking, and golfing together. We were "big shots" in the company and would "live it up" on business trips. But now that I was a Christian, I didn't want to do that anymore. Of course, he didn't like that idea!

When he called, he knew I was going off on some "God told me" idea that was not according to policy. He asked me why I was shuttling in all these cars and what my reservation count was. He finally asked me "Why are you getting these cars?"
I knew I was sunk. I told him. "The Lord told me." That was it. I, of all people, knew the reservation system and company policy and knew I had no reason to shuttle in cars. He had me. He told me that he would call me Saturday morning and "discuss this again."

I knew my job was on the line. This was his chance to get rid of me. I was devastated. All that Friday afternoon, more and more cars arrived. Some of the drivers were even laughing because word got out that I didn't know what I was doing. Nobody shuttles in cars on Fridays. Nobody!

That evening, I pulled up the reservation manifest and saw nothing. I didn't even need these cars for Monday. I would have to have the expense of sending these cars back to other airports at a cost to my airport. What have I done? I am sunk!

I stayed on at the airport that Friday night. I even sent the last rental agent home early. I would meet the final arrivals myself. The reports for Saturday and Sunday showed no cars needed. I had listened and acted on what I thought "God told me." I knew Saturday morning would be my last day at Avis.

The last plane arrived that night on schedule at 11:00pm. People got off, went to the different car rental counters and some came to mine. I fixed them up and smiled, but I knew this was the last for me.

The other rental car agents closed up their counters, shut off the lights and went home. They smiled (or should I say smirked) as they walked by. They had seen all the cars coming in and it was the talk of all the car rental companies. The airport was now quiet, just a few people finishing up for the night. What a drag. . .

It was then that I heard the sound of a jet engine spooling down. As I looked down the concourse, I could see dozens of people walking with attaché cases. These weren't tourist. These were businesspeople.

All the rental companies were closed, and their staff gone, all of these people came to the only car rental counter that was still open, mine. They were all going to need cars for a secret government meeting. They were not supposed to make reservations so that no one would know that they were coming. The meeting was going to last for 2 weeks! As I was filling out rental agreements for the people lined up at the counter, another jet spooled down outside the terminal! More government people for the same meeting!

When I was through, I did not have a single car to left to rent. I had brought in the correct number - - - - - Scratch that, "the Lord had provided" the exact number of cars that He needed! In fact, I didn't have a car left for me to take home except for one that was "out of service" because of a faulty power window!

The next morning, I got the call from the district manager who informed me that my actions were going to be reviewed and this would be a problem for me. I had to interrupt him and tell him, "I'm glad you called, I am going to need more cars to meet my Monday morning reservations!"

Matthew 6:8 *for your Father knoweth what things ye have need of, before ye ask him.*

Chapter 8   No limitations

Romans 10:17 *So then faith cometh by hearing, and hearing by the word of God.*

There is an old song in the Hymnals called, "It is no Secret."

"It is no secret, what God can do.
What he's done for others,
He can do for you."

I desire to share what I've seen the Lord do. I know He is no respecter of person.

Hebrews 11:6 *But without faith it is impossible to please him: for he that cometh to God must believe that he is, and that he is a rewarder of them that diligently seek him.*

I can say that I was very fortunate that I didn't have anyone to question about what God would or would not do. I wasn't taught limitations of what or what not to ask. So I had to learn from the Lord. Now this statement, in itself, is not an endorsement to just do whatever you want without any leadership or accountability to others. I can say that I had a sincere desire to serve the Lord.

I found a Pentecostal Church and went every time the doors were open. I would go to Church Sunday morning, take a nap during the afternoon and then go to the evening service that night. After Church, I would go right to bed and sleep till morning. I really took the Lord at his word that Sunday was a "day of rest". The staff at the office on Monday was always wondering where I got all the energy from.

Exodus 23:12 *Six days thou shalt do thy work, and on the seventh day thou shalt rest:*

The Lord blessed our business, several of the staff renewed their walk in the Lord. One of the rental agents, Mary Jo, even got bold enough in the Lord to pray with folks at the counter before they went on their way. We put the Lord first and the Lord blessed.

Luke 12:31 *But rather seek ye the kingdom of God; and all these things shall be added unto you.*

Instead of going to rock concerts and other types of trips, I would go to Birmingham or Atlanta to different Church meetings and conventions. In Atlanta, I went to a service where a man from Tennessee named H. Richard Hall, was holding service. I remember he told me that he "saw me standing beside the road hitch hiking, in 90 days." I appreciated his prayer, but he didn't know that I always had the best of company cars and personal cars and flew to many different places.

Chapter 9   The young rich man

Matthew 19:29 *And every one that hath forsaken houses, or brethren, or sisters, or father, or mother, or wife, or children, or lands, for my name's sake, shall receive an hundredfold, and shall inherit everlasting life.*

The Lord will put a challenge or a test before you. We don't know who we are or how strong we are until we are tested or tried. We can either accept the challenge or always wonder if we could live up to the challenge.

One evening, while reading the Bible, I came across the scriptures of the young rich man. It is in Mathew chapter 19. He told Jesus how he was leading a good life, but asked what he should do to inherit eternal life.

Matthew 19:21 *Jesus said unto him, If thou wilt be perfect, go and* **sell that thou hast,** *and* **give to the poor,** *and thou shalt have treasure in heaven: and* **come and follow me.**

When I read this, I wondered, do you take the Bible as a history book? Or do you take it as a road map to where you are going? Maybe you take it as an inspiration book. But as I read this scripture, I saw that it was a junction in life for this young rich man. It was an example for the next person to either follow or ignore. The young man heard what Jesus said to him and he had a choice.

Matthew 19:22 *But when the young man heard that saying, he went away sorrowful: for he had great possessions.*

He made his choice and immediately was sorrowful, yet he stayed with his choice. All the things that he had done up to this time was religious, but now, Jesus wanted him to follow and have a relationship with the young man.

As I read the scripture and understood the question that Jesus gave the man, the man's decision would change his life. I now stood in the same question, what would be my choice? I had a fine job with a great future, I had no bills, I didn't have a family that was dependent on me, I was young and in good health, what would be my choice?

I thought about it and decided to find out what would happen if I would take the Bible and Jesus' teachings at his word.

Chapter 10   Come and follow me

I notified the district office that I was putting in my resignation and would work it out after I trained a new manager. It was a shock to a lot of people even in the Church that I attended. They then suggested that I attend the Church's Bible College, but I didn't want to go that way again. I wanted to trust what the Bible said, literally trust the Bible.

All the things that I had acquired, I found a person that I could give it to that would mean something to them. Some of what I had, I gave to folks that couldn't afford to buy. It was a time of fulfilling the scripture:

Matthew 19:21 *Jesus said unto him, If thou wilt be perfect, go and sell that thou hast, and give to the poor, and thou shalt have treasure in heaven: and come and follow me.*

That weekend our Church was having a Revival with a singing group. The singing group was Nancy Harmon with the backup group called the Victory Voices. They didn't have a drummer in the group, and I knew how to play the drums, so it seemed like God knew the needs and I was going to fill it. But the revival came and went, and nothing happened. It was a pretty discouraging thing. Did God let me down? Did I choose to follow some dream that wasn't real? Did I take this "Bible thing" too far? Maybe the Bible wasn't supposed to be taken literally. I had sold my car, emptied my apartment, finished training the new manager that they flew in, I wondered what was I to do?

I was now homeless, without a job and without a direction to go!

My former secretary told me that H. Richard Hall, the Preacher that I met in Atlanta, was going to be at a Church down in Melbourne Florida about 450 miles away. So, the new Airport Manager told to me to just take a car and shuttle it down to the airport in Melbourne for him. Great! So, with all my possessions in a backpack, I hopped in the car and took off for Melbourne.

I found the Church where the meeting was at and then drove on to the airport to drop off the car. It wasn't that far back to the Church, so I put my stuff down beside me on the curb and put my thumb out to catch a ride.

As I stood there, I remembered being at a Church service in Atlanta when the Minister told me that he saw me "standing beside the road, hitch hiking, with your bags packed, it will be in 90 days"! When I got to the Church, I found a calendar and figured it out. It was exactly 90 days from the day when the Minister told me to this day that I was in Melbourne!

Chapter 11   Our Steps are Ordered

I walked into the Church, it wasn't locked. It was a different Church than I was used to. It had a baptism pool in the front and had a scripture written on it that said.

Act_8:36 *See, here is water; what doth hinder me to be baptized?*

What perfect timing! I had been reading the Bible and one thing that I hoped that I could do was get Baptized again. I knew that I had been sprinkled and dedicated when I was a baby, but now that I know the Lord and I am accountable for my own decisions, I wanted to get baptized again.

Now, I understood that before, I believed in God, that he existed, that he was "out there, somewhere". But before, I had "religion" and not a "relationship" with God.

John 3:5 *Jesus answered, Verily, verily, I say unto thee, Except a man be born of water and of the Spirit, he cannot enter into the kingdom of God.*

John 3:7 *Marvel not that I said unto thee, Ye must be born again.*

I knew that I had been "born again" when I prayed at the airport. My life was totally changed.

John 14:1 *Let not your heart be troubled: ye believe in God, believe also in me.*

Then there was one scripture that says it all.

John 14:6 *Jesus saith unto him, **I am the way, the truth, and the life: no man cometh unto the Father, but by me.***

I had been reading a lot in the New Testament and especially in the book of Acts. I saw how that the Book of Acts is talking about the

Church after the death and resurrection of Jesus. It was and is the continuation of what Christianity is to be. I noticed that every baptism in the New Testament, the person was Baptized "In the Name of Jesus".

I really knew that I was forgiven and a new person on the inside. I knew that God had washed away my sins and that I wanted to be clean on the inside and outside.

Hebrews 10:22 *Let us draw near with a true heart in full assurance of faith, having our hearts sprinkled from an evil conscience, and our bodies washed with pure water.*

It was so easy to see that salvation came from repenting to Jesus

Well the pastor, Bro. Joel Velie, came out from his office and we met. I told him why I came here and commented on his Baptistery. I told him that I wanted to get baptized now that I am a Christian. Well he liked that! He started to give me a teaching on how he believed; I kind of stopped him and told him what I had been reading and how I wanted it done. He was really pleased; it was exactly as he believed and taught.

That night as the service was going on, it seemed the service came to a halt. I was wanting to get baptized so I hopped it would happen tonight. So, the Revival Preacher said that there was someone here that was wanting to get baptized tonight. Of course, I knew that was me. So I went up and told him it was me and I wanted to be Baptized according to the scripture:

Acts 2:38 *Then Peter said unto them, Repent, and be baptized every one of you in the name of Jesus Christ for the remission of sins, and ye shall receive the gift of the Holy Ghost.*

The Lord had already given me the "Holy Ghost" in my bedroom, so I wanted to complete the scripture.

It was great! I now knew I had fulfilled the scripture in my life that was undone. You know, when you do what is right, it sets an example of others to follow? That night, others went up to get baptized again and renew their vows to God. In fact, 150 people came up, It was like pulling fish out of a lake! People were shouting and praising God. Never had this Church seen any meeting like this!

Chapter 12   The Extra-Long Years.

The Revival came and went. I had now no place to go, but the Minister of the revival was going back to his headquarters in Cleveland, Tennessee. I caught a ride with one of the young men name Dewy Esquinance, who was "following" the ministry.

The Minister was H. Richard Hall. He had an evangelistic Ministry that traveled across the southeast. Putting up Gospel Tents in small towns, preaching in Churches, and buildings to large and small crowds, his ministry touched many people with a traditional Pentecostal message.

Bro Hall, as everybody called him, was individual to behold. Always wore a black suit, black tie, and a white shirt. He could have easily been mistaken for Johnny Cash, and he shared the same poor upbringing that made him the person into what he was.

Bro. Hall wasn't very excited to have me hanging around. His plan was to have a bunch of "hippies" or Jesus freaks, travel with him wherever he preached at and I didn't look much like a hippie. He told me he didn't need me so go back and get a job.   But Bro Hall let me sleep on the couch in his home. I ended up spending several months in home with Bro. Hall and Sis. Hall and traveled each week with him to his revivals. I started doing most of the driving for him and did this for several years. We covered 100,000 miles a year from Maryland to Texas, Florida to Wisconsin, and each weekend somewhere preaching.

Bro Hall had his "inner circle" of people. Mike, Pat and Kent were the three "Hippies" that he always called on to testify and preach in his services. Bro Hall couldn't remember my name, so one day he called me "Extra Long" and it just stuck. Others joined along the way, David and Dennis Jenkins, Sandy Pfeiffer, Pat Hayes, David Drueding, Gary Church, Mike Ferree, Becky Ferree, Charlotte Murray, Polly Hilton, Marsha Graff, the Rogers family and so many more that joined in the youth group.

The organist of the group was Don Warren. He played a Hammond B3 that really moved a service along. I took up with Don and started playing the drums with him. It was interesting, I always wanted to play in a "rock band" and travel around the country back when I was a "sinner", but now here I was with the chance to do this "for the Lord".

It truly was amazing and there were so many people that I met during the 12 years that I was a part of the United Christian Church.

I eventually bought an old 1966 Chevy van with my tax refund for $400. I put an old cot in it and with some green bed sheets for curtains; I made it into my "home". I bought a "die hard" battery from Sears, put an 8-track tape player in it and listened to Alexander Scourby read the Bible for the Blind every night. It would play over and over all night long. If there was a scripture that I really needed to hear, I would "wake up" just in time to hear that scripture once again. All told, I lived in a van for about 7 years, it was nothing to just pull over on the side of the road or at rest stop along the interstate and sleep for the night. Alexander would "read me to sleep".

I met some wonderful people thru the years and watched God move mightily in and out of service. The Reids, the Crumps, the Crowleys, the Stienkes, the Brocks and so many other dear friends, they became family to me over the years.

Mark 10:29 *And Jesus answered and said, Verily I say unto you,*

There is no man that hath left house, or brethren, or sisters, or father, or mother, or wife, or children, or lands, for my sake, and the gospel's,

Mark 10:30 *But he shall receive an hundredfold now in this time, houses, and brethren, and sisters, and mothers, and children, and lands, with persecutions; and in the world to come eternal life.*

Chapter 13   Seek ye first the kingdom of God

Matthew 6:6 *But thou, when thou prayest, enter into thy closet, and when thou hast shut thy door, pray to thy Father which is in secret; and thy Father which seeth in secret shall reward thee openly.*

Brother Hall had made some bunk beds in the back of the Church for the "youth group" to stay in for the summer when we were all back in Cleveland. I stayed in one of the bunk beds for a while. It was ok, we had good fellowship with the group, but I really missed my private time reading and praying in my van. I remember thinking that I want to go back sleeping in the van, but I really did need a good mattress.

The next evening, I left out for Orlando Florida where the revival was going to be that following day. I drove through Atlanta, Georgia and then stopped in a rest area in southern part of the state for the night.

The next morning, I finished the drive down to the Church and got there about 5:30 pm for the 7:30 pm Service. There was already a car in the parking lot. I went over to speak with the people. It was a lady that would come to services known to everyone as Sister Thompson. I didn't know her very well, but she always seemed like a very good praying person.

She asked how the "youth group" was doing and asked me if they could use anything. I told her that anything would be fine. She said that she had brought some things in the back of her car. So, we went to unload the stuff to put in my van to be taken to Cleveland. She told me that she had brought a mattress.

As I walked to the back of the car to help her get the mattress out, I remembered the night before when I told the Lord that I wanted to go back to sleeping in the van. I asked Sis. Thompson, "This mattress wouldn't be long and skinny like me would it?"

She laughed and said "Yes, it is."

I asked her, "Would you mind if I used it myself?"

She told me. "That would be fine. Yesterday, the Lord told me to buy a mattress. I went to the store and saw this one on sale. It is over 6' long and about 2' wide. So, I bought it and brought it tonight."

I took it to the van. It was a perfect fit from the back of the front seat to the back of the van and it was the perfect width. It even was green colored to match the green curtains.

Now you may say that I found a great way to pray for "things", but I got much more than that. The real gift that I got was her faith and her understanding of the Lord's will in our lives.

Think of this. She felt the Lord speaking to her to buy a mattress, then she went to a store, finding this weird size mattress on sale, buying it and then taking it to Church with her the next day. Who would do something like this? How many times have you bought a mattress to take to Church?

When I told others about how this happened, they asked me to pray for someone to give them stuff. They missed the whole idea of the blessing! They wanted the power of prayer to receive and not intercede. Finding God's will for others is the real power of prayer and then putting action to those prayers is God's will.

Oh yes, I got a mattress, but I got so much more of a desire to help others.

Matthew 6:33 *But seek ye first the kingdom of God, and his righteousness; and all these things shall be added unto you.*

Chapter 14   **Like Precious Faith**

2Peter1:1 *Simon Peter, a servant and an apostle of Jesus Christ, to them that have obtained like precious faith with us through the righteousness of God and our Saviour Jesus Christ:*

There is a difference in being a religious person to being a person that has a personal relationship with the Lord. A relationship is something you have by taking time to be with someone.

> **Matthew 8:19-20** *And a certain scribe came, and said unto him, Master, I will follow thee whithersoever thou goest.*
> *And Jesus saith unto him, The foxes have holes, and the birds of the air have nests; but the Son of man hath not where to lay his head.*

The scribe was trying to relate to Jesus that he was so devoted that he would go everywhere with Jesus. But to walk daily with someone, means to understand that person. See life like that person sees life. Share the thoughts, share understanding, share cares.

To really understand what it means to be a Christian, is to understand that you are part of the body of Christ. Born again into His kingdom. Do you believe that the scribe understood this? The scribe was telling Jesus that wherever he went, wherever he slept, he wanted to be there, with Jesus. But to walk with Jesus doesn't mean that were he goes, you go. It doesn't mean where he sleeps, you sleep.

> **Matthew 8:20** *And Jesus saith unto him, The foxes have holes, and the birds of the air have nests; but the Son of man hath not where to lay his head.*

But Jesus was looking for a body to place his head on. We are to be the body of Christ; he wants to be the head of the Body.

Colossians 1:18 *And he is the head of the body, the church: who is the beginning, the firstborn from the dead; that in all things he might have the preeminence.*

Sometimes when I pray, I tell the Lord, if he wants to have a body to follow his will, use me. Not for glory, but for service. Picture if you would, a puppet. It has no self-will, it only does what the puppeteer wants it to do.

What about our lives? Do you only do what you want to do? Are you self-willed? What if you let the Lord pull your strings? How more productive would your life be for Him.

Matthew 7:21 *Not every one that saith unto me, Lord, Lord, shall enter into the kingdom of heaven; but he that doeth the will of my Father which is in heaven.*

Philippians 2:3-5 *Let nothing be done through strife or vainglory; but in lowliness of mind let each esteem other better than themselves.*
Look not every man on his own things, but every man also on the things of others.
Let this mind be in you, which was also in Christ Jesus:

So, having the mind of Christ Jesus. Not my will, but thine be done. This is walking with the Lord. This is what having a relationship with the Lord is.

Back to the thoughts of the young ruler. He knew what it was to do religious things.

Matthew 19: 20 *The young man saith unto him, All these things have I kept from my youth up: what lack I yet?*

But what the young man was lacking, was to realize that Jesus had accepted the young man and asked him to leave all and follow him. Be a friend to Jesus, go with Him, follow Him.

And the young man couldn't do it.

Chapter 15   Follow me

Matthew 4:19 *And he saith unto them Follow me, and I will make fishers of men.*

The 12 years that I worked with the United Christian Church, I put my business skills to work.   We were starting a correspondence Bible School.   Several of the other ministers that had joined the work began to write the lessons.   Pat Hayes, Kent Sullivan and Mike Shreve were the principal ministers compiling the studies.   The other people in the office, like Lita Peru Esquinance, were printing the lessons out on an old mimeograph machine. But I saw that we needed to print these lessons out for a larger growth.

So, we built a printing shop with used equipment.   Little by little we bought a printing press, a camera and plate maker for the printing press and then a typesetting machine.   Old by today's standard, but good enough for us to get the job done.   Nobody amongst us had any background in doing this except for the scripture.

Philippians 4:13 *I can do all things through Christ which strengtheneth me.*

What started out as an "idea" grew to a printing shop that printed gospel literature to thousands of students around the world studying the Bible.

I believe that the best statement that can be made to an individual who wants to do something for the Lord is the following scriptures.

Zechariah 4:10 *For who hath despised the day of small things?*

Too many times a person thinks that the "real" work of the Lord is in the pulpit leading a song service or being the minister preaching the "word of the Lord".   But there is always something that needs to be done that is truly the Lord's work. Nothing that you do for the Lord is a small thing.

Ecclesiastes 8:9 *All this have I seen, and applied my heart unto every work that is done under the sun:*

Chapter 16   Send forth labourers into his harvest.

Luke 10:2 *Therefore said he unto them, The harvest truly is great, but the labourers are few: pray ye therefore the Lord of the harvest, that he would send forth labourers into his harvest.*

The youth group that Bro Hall envisioned, was starting to come together. Different people from around the country were coming in and joining the group to work through the summer. They came from Texas, Louisiana, Florida, Maryland, etc., across the southeast United States

We were in service in Central Florida. I had my '66 Chevy van that I was now my home and I was traveling in. We had just finished up services and our next revival was in Maryland.

Sandy Pfeiffer was riding with me at the time, he was from Louisiana. He and some of his friends in that area had a "Jesus Coffee shop" where there would be music and sharing the Gospel to those who came in. Sandy and I were in Florida for one of the meetings with Bro. Hall. Bro Hall was going to Maryland next, so we needed to get there. We checked the money that we had between us and there was not enough to make it to Maryland. So, we stopped in a 7-11 store and Sandy went in to prepay the gasoline.

As I waited outside, it was kind of tough to know that we wouldn't have enough money, but we would just go by "faith". As Sandy walked out of the 7-11, I noticed a bag of something that he was carrying. When I asked him, he said, "Well, I knew we didn't have enough money to make it, so I bought some grape juice and crackers so we could have communion."

I couldn't believe that he did that! We needed everything for the gas! What was he thinking? Now, how were we supposed to get there? We now had enough gas for 350 miles of the 950-mile trip and no money left over. We pulled over to the side of the lot and got in the back of the van and had communion with the grape juice and crackers.

46

We really did feel the presence of the Lord and felt ok about the problem that we were facing.

It was getting late afternoon when we decided to get started to see what was going to happen. Sandy remembered someone that he knew who lived in Orlando, about 50 miles away. He figured that we could stop by and get something to eat. That sounded ok to me.

As we turned down the cull de sac that his friend lived in, we noticed a fellow setting on a duffle bag by the curb. It was his friend, David Drueding. David had been a Marine stationed in Okinawa, Japan for 3 years. He was All Marine Corps Judo Champion in 1971. While in the service, he had received the "Holy Ghost". When he came home, his father didn't like that. He was given an ultimatum from his dad to "either get rid of that Holy Ghost or move out of the house." So, David packed his belongings into his Marine duffle bag and moved out to the curb. He prayed for the Lord to help him to see what the Lord was going to do next.

And here we are pulling up to his house. He told us of the problem that he was in. So, I told him we were traveling with a Minister and were heading up to Maryland for services this coming weekend and he was more than welcome to join us. Of course, my next question was, "Do you have any money?"

He had some, but he suggested that we visit some friends of his in Winter Park. He said they might fix us a meal. That did sound good because we had a long way to drive yet.

The Steinke's home was in Winter Park, Florida. As we pulled up to the house, we were warmly greeted by them and then asked to stay for dinner (Praise God!). After dinner we fellowshipped for a while, but in my heart, I knew that we were going to have to get on the road to Maryland. As we started to go, Colleen Steinkie demanded "in the Name of Jesus" that we stay the night. Well, I wasn't going leave if she was that determined.

As we sat at the table and fellowshipped about the Lord, there was a knock on the door. The Steinke's had 3 daughters in High School and a son in grade school. At the door was one of their friends that "just happened" to stop by. A few minutes later, another knock on the door and more friends stop in. Within a half hours' time, 21 teenagers stopped by for no reason at all. So here we are with a family that we didn't know, with a living room full of teenage kids. So, Sandy got out his guitar and told them "We are Jesus freaks and the Lord sent you here tonight so you could hear about Jesus." We sang songs and we shared our testimony of what the Lord has done in our lives and then we shared Jesus with them and His great love. When the service was over, 17 of the kids prayed for the Lord to forgive them of theirs sins. The next day 5 of the kids came back and we baptized them in the Name of Jesus in the pool behind the house.

The outreach was growing in the Orlando area. They were having prayer meetings every Thursday morning. The crowd grew so large that they thought about tearing out walls in their home to accommodate the people. So, Colleen Steinke rented the Civic Center in Winter Park to meet the demand. Many mission trips around the world were conducted by members from this group. Each week, there would be as many as 300 people come to the prayer meeting. Colleen Steinke started many people in their work in the Lord.

Before Sister Colleen passed away, she and her daughters, Mary Derringer and Michelle Hagel inspired people in the Lord.

Bro David Drueding ended up spending the next 30 years teaching English in schools all around the world from the Philippines, Saudi Arabia, Cambodia, England, Korea, China, Malaysia, Hong Kong, Iraq and Japan. Dave passed away in Cambodia. I believe it was years of drinking water in these different countries. It was a sad day when they posted a picture of the roadside crematory in Toul Kork, Cambodia where David was cremated.

And all this from him setting on his duffle bag wondering what the Lord was going to do with him.

I can also remember the lost and hopeless feeling we had when we only had enough gas to get us to where the Lord wanted us to be that day.

Mark 1:17 *And Jesus said unto them, Come ye after me, and I will make you to become fishers of men.*

Chapter 17   **Late one night!**

I was always amazed what the Lord would do to reach a soul.

1 Corinthians 12:7 *But the manifestation of the Spirit is given to every man to profit withal.*

I was in Asheville North Carolina, and after church I went to a 7-11 store to get a Mountain Dew and a Hershey Bar. It was late that night, and across the parking lot I could see a bunch of motorcycles parked in the dark with all the riders around them. These weren't the expensive fancy ones like you see today. No, this was a much "rougher" group of riders on some really "bad" bikes.

I felt the Lord speak to my heart and tell me to go talk with these guys. As I went into the store and got my stuff, one of the bikers was in front of me at the checkout line. He glanced at me and I glanced at him and I said "Hey, how are you doing?" He said "Hey" back, and that was the end of that.

I thought, "Lord, you wanted me to talk to them, I did." But as I was walking back to my van in the parking lot, I realize that the Lord really wanted me to talk to them. So, I turned around and started backed for the group. The Bible says,

Ecclesiastes 9:10 *Whatsoever thy hand findeth to do, do it with all thy might;"*

Well, I didn't. As I was walking toward the group, instead of walking up real bold like, I was kind of shuffling my feet wondering what I was going to say. I didn't see the empty soda can as my foot accidentally kicked the can and it flew towards the bikes.

Have you ever had an out of body experience? My whole body was reaching for that can!!! "NOoooo.....!!!!"

The can flew into the pack of bikes and hit one of the motorcycles in the spokes. All the bikers turned and looked at me. 6' 6" 175 lbs. With a shirt and a tie on, on a Saturday night, kicking a can at their bikes. Saturday night was now going to get interesting!

They came toward me as I was walking toward them. They gathered around me and were going to start something. After all, I was the one that started it, they were going to finish it.

I knew I had to get this going, so I told them, "Look, the Lord told me to talk to you guys."

Oh, that went over well. Now they were making fun, trying to push me, wanting to get something going on a Saturday night. I told them, "The Lord is dealing with someone tonight."

It wasn't looking good for me. When all of the sudden, from the motorcycles, one of the bikers said, "Leave him alone!"

That sounded good.

The guy said, "Leave him alone. I'm the one he is here for." "I'm backslid. I used to be the youth director of our Church."

The guys turned to him as a friend. No more were they bad bikers, but now they were friends wondering what he said. He began to tell them that he had been the youth director of the Church and that he had quit Church and turned from God. He told them he knew that the Lord had sent him this guy to tell him to "get right" with God.

I told them that we need to make this happen and we prayed together. As we prayed, the man opened up his heart and truly prayed. If any of his friends ever wondered what it was like to hear someone pray, they heard it now from this man who was humbling his heart and asking for forgiveness. It was wonderful!

After we were thru praying, he started telling his friends about the Lord, telling them how great the Lord had been in his life, and how good it was to feel him again. It was like a Church was starting amongst these guys.

I was like, "well guys, I got to go..." but it really didn't matter, God raised up a leader in this group to tell them of His coming. They were having Church, on a parking lot of a 7-11, around a bunch of bikes, with a bunch of men who really realized what is important in life.

Note: Don't go kicking cans thinking God is in it!

Chapter 18   **Other Men's labor.**

It is important to remember that when you take the time to share with someone about Jesus, whatever you tell them about Him, He will confirm his word with signs and wonders. The sign or gift is for the person that the Lord wants to bless.

Hebrews 2:4 *God also bearing them witness, both with signs and wonders, and with divers miracles, and gifts of the Holy Ghost, according to his own will?*

I was in Birmingham Alabama. We were in service in Bessemer, Alabama, so I decided to go over to the University of Alabama and witness to people on campus. I talked to several students and saw one student setting on the curbside.

I went over to her and sat down on the curb and just started off by asking, "Are you a Christian?"

She said "no."

It seemed a little strange that she didn't rebuff me for asking, so I continued by telling her that sin separates us from God and the only way to know God is to ask him to forgive us of our sin.

Still no rebuff from her.

I began to wonder if this was a trap or something. I have talked with people before that would want to argue or justify themselves or any number of things, but she just kept on listening.

I told her that Jesus went to the Cross, was crucified, dead and buried, and on the third day, he was resurrected from the dead. He promised that whosoever believeth in him should have everlasting life.

She still seemed to receive what I was saying, so I asked her if she wanted to pray with me and ask the Lord to forgive her of her sin.

She said "Yes".

I had never seen anyone so "open" to the Gospel.

We prayed for several minutes and tears dropped from her eyes onto the payment. When we finished praying, you could see that the "burden" that she was carrying had been lifted.

Her tears of grief changed to tears with laughter. Something had happened and she knew it.

I told her that I had never seen anyone so "open and willing" to listen to a person share the Gospel and pray before.

She said that about an hour before, someone had approached her and started to share about "Jesus" to her. She said that she "cussed them out". She made fun of them and ran them off. She said as those people left, it was as if "everything good in my life left me."

She said that she felt so bad for what she had done, that she sat down on the sidewalk and in a little prayer to herself, asked God to give her another chance.

About that time, I came along.

As far as I am concerned, those first Christians that witnessed to her, might have felt bad for the way she treated them, but God in his mercy, sent another messenger. It was a sign to this girl that God really did care for her and also gave her another chance.

John 4:38 *I sent you to reap that whereon ye bestowed no labour: other men laboured, and ye are entered into their labours.*

Chapter 19 God will make a way.

1 Corinthians 10:13 *There hath no temptation taken you but such as is common to man: but God is faithful, who will not suffer you to be tempted above that ye are able; but will with the temptation also make a way to escape, that ye may be able to bear it.*

I was on my way to a revival in Florida. I so remember that as I checked how much money I had; I didn't have enough to make it. The Church that I was working with would give me a little money each week. But as I used what I had; it would always be gone by the end of the week.

I believe that this was an interesting trial. I had more than enough money when I was with working at Avis, it was easy to believe how God would meet your needs when you have a lot of money. But it is different when you don't know where the next dollar is going to come from.

We can read about the disciples when they were in the boat in the middle of a storm.

Mark 4:37-40 *And there arose a great storm of wind, and the waves beat into the ship, so that it was now full.*
And he was in the hinder part of the ship, asleep on a pillow: and they awake him, and say unto him, Master, carest thou not that we perish?
And he arose, and rebuked the wind, and said unto the sea, Peace, be still. And the wind ceased, and there was a great calm.
And he said unto them, Why are ye so fearful? how is it that ye have no faith?

There is a difference in crying out to God when your need is so great, than it is to cry out to God because you don't believe he hears you.

God cares for His. The very hairs of your head are numbered. There is not a storm that you have, or are or will be going through, that the Lord hasn't made a way to escape.

The disciples where **on the boat** with Jesus but **not in the boat** with Jesus. You can be around Christian people but never be in your place with Jesus.

You can sit in a garage all day and never become an automobile, and you can sit in a Church all day and never become a believer.

But here is the difference in having the Holy Ghost in your personal life. The Bible teaches us this.

> **Jude 1:20** *But ye, beloved,* **building up yourselves on your most holy faith, praying in the Holy Ghost,**

As I counted the money that I had, I had a choice. I could put everything that I had in the gas tank and would make it to the Church in Florida. But it would be really close, in fact, I wouldn't have enough to eat anything on the way.

The other choice was, if I stopped to get something to eat, I wouldn't have enough gas to get to the Church. So, here was the problem. Does God care for me more than the van? If I stopped along the way and ate a meal, somewhere in the morning I would run out of gas. No problem though, I could just hitch hike from wherever the van stops on to the Church. I figured it would be maybe 80 miles short, but that was not bad.

Or, I could just proclaim a fast and drive on, but I really was hungry. In fact, the more I thought about it, the hungrier I got. I decided that God cared for me more than the piece of metal that I was driving that was my home. I stopped at a restaurant at the next exit ramp on the interstate.

It was a fish and chicken fast food place just off the interstate, in fact, is was a brand-new Captain D's. The store was clean, the people were bright and cheery, and they had no idea of the problem that I was in. A full stomach verses a full tank of gas. But as I looked at the glowing menu on the wall behind the counter, I could see bundles of fish with fries, or 2 pieces of fish with fries and coleslaw. 2 pieces of fish might mean that I would get 100 miles from the Church before the gas runs out. But if I have to hitch hike, I would rather hitch hike on a full stomach.

I ordered the 2-piece meal. As I sat down, I got a paper and read the news (like it really mattered) so I would have something of the world to think on.

I thanked the Lord for the food. The meal was really good. It was worth the sacrifice that I would face come morning, but as I came to the last bite, I really knew that this was not going to "fill me up". It was kind of sad. Knowing that I wasn't full, wasn't going to make it to the Church, knowing that maybe I should have just fasted.

As I opened my mouth for the last piece of fish: there, in the crusty batter of the fish, was a fly. Petrified in the batter! What are the odds of a fly landing on a piece of fish just as they dropped it into the boiling grease! Insult to injury! My last bite of fish! Well, the Lord giveth, and the Lord taketh away.

I cleaned off my table, pick up the tray and started to dump it in the container. One of the eager people behind the counter, "How was your meal?" I told them "it was very good."

But you know, **what are** the chances of a fly landing on a piece of fish just as it goes in the boiling grease? So, I stopped to show them the petrified fly. Poor thing.

They were so embarrassed! I didn't mean to embarrass them. It was just a freak accident. Well, they said. What did you order? I told them it was the 2-piece fish with fries and coleslaw. They said, "Get him another order!" I was shocked and told them they didn't have to do that. They insisted. So, I got a double portion of dinner. I sat down and thanked the Lord again for meeting the need.

As I was enjoying this meal, more than anyone would ever know, the manager came over to me to apologized again for the mistake. I told them to please not worry that I was fine and thanked them again for doing what they had done.

The manager insisted that he would give me my money back and this meal would be on the house! Some people will never know what it means to be thankful!

Matthew 6:8 *Be not ye therefore like unto them: for your Father knoweth what things ye have need of, before ye ask him.*

P.S. I made it to the Church.

Chapter 20   Fasting

So, you have made it this far in this book. That's good. I really debated with myself on about putting this next topic in the book. Fasting.

I started a fast one morning. Just felt like doing it. I took my shower, washed my face, put on my clothes and started out the day with me and my secret before the Lord.

> **Matthew 6:17-18** *But thou, when thou fastest, anoint thine head, and wash thy face;*
> *That thou appear not unto men to fast, but unto thy Father which is in secret: and thy Father, which seeth in secret, shall reward thee openly.*

I decided to only drink water on this fast. I made it through the first day and the next morning thought about going another day. So, I did. The second day I knew that one more day would make it a 3-day fast and that I had not done one in a long time. It was not easy. I think that there are a lot of toxins and junk that gets out of your system that makes going on a 3 day fast difficult.

The morning of the 4th day was nice. It was a good feeling to know that I had made it for 3 days and nights on this fast and I had done it in secret. It was good to know that a good breakfast would be awesome!

I was working in the printing office the first part of the week, then we would leave out for a revival over the weekend or off to a tent revival or Church revival somewhere. I would have only a limited time in each place, so nobody would really be able to see that I was fasting. That made it much easier.

So here I was on the 4th day. A seven day fast would be a good personal goal to reach for. I decided to include drinks on this fast. I believe that anything that you sacrifice before the Lord is accepted of him. I would start the morning with a Welch's Grape juice. Maybe I would drink an orange juice later in the day.

Well 4 days became 7 days. I really praised God that I had gone 7 days. But at 7 days, you are only 3 days away from a 10 day fast. I know that I will never be this close to 10 days so why stop now.

This fast was for me and everyone else that really wanted to fast but could not. So as far as I was concerned, everyone that prayed and encouraged me, they also got the blessing with me.

I saw the Lord work in mighty ways during the fast. People were blessed, they would ask me to pray about things for them and God answered. But let me tell you what I saw. God is the one who answers prayers. People believed and God answered. It is a simple as that.

Matthew 17:20 *And Jesus said unto them, Because of your unbelief: for verily I say unto you, If ye have faith as a grain of mustard seed, ye shall say unto this mountain, Remove hence to yonder place; and it shall remove; and **nothing shall be impossible** unto you.*

Hebrews11:6 *But without faith it is impossible to please him: for he that cometh to God must believe that he is, and that he is a rewarder of them that diligently seek him.*

See, it wasn't the fast that brought them the blessing, it was faith that it would happen.

Mark 11:24 *Therefore I say unto you, What things soever ye desire, when ye pray, believe that ye receive them, and ye shall have them.*

Chapter 21   Fasting, Day 10 on

10 days put me halfway to a 21 day fast. I had never been this far before. I knew that I would never be there again or let's say that I would have to fast 10 days just to get where I am now. It would be easier just to keep on going because I had come so far.

It was starting to get obvious that I was on a fast. It was hard to hide it. I had now lost about 15 pounds, didn't go out to eat with friends after Church. Food really does smell so good when you get this far in a fast. Your senses become more acute, you can drive down a road on a Sunday afternoon and just about tell what was being cooked in each house. Chicken there, roast beef at that home, mashed potatoes and gravy over there, you just become more sensitive.

As I approached the 21st day, I was thankful that I had made it. It took the Lord. God would have been pleased with a One Day fast. But I had an opportunity to do something that many Christians would want to do. But they would have a job and a family that they needed to put first. That doesn't mean that I am closer to the Lord than them, I just had opportunity to do this.

Galatians 6:10 *As we have therefore opportunity, let us do good unto all men, especially unto them who are of the household of faith.*

I have seen where ministers position themselves to be great men as if someone working a job or caring of their family, supporting their pastor, or some other "worldly" adventure, made them a lesser person. Shame on that attitude! Every man will have his reward.

Many of the group knew that I was on a fast. Word got out to people coming to the revivals. But now I was in a dilemma. I am now over halfway to a 40 day fast. If I quit now, God would still be pleased with my fast. But if I quit and decided to try this later, I would have to fast 21 days to get here again. Hmmm.

Then there was another matter, and of course, it includes food. Every year we would go to the Full Gospel Church of God camp meeting in Carbon Hill Alabama. I always looked forward to this weeklong service. There was preaching morning, afternoon and evening service. But beside that, there was free breakfast, lunch and dinner served every day. Lots of fellowship, lots of good food and great services.

I would be there, but the 7-day camp meeting would be on the last 7 days of my 40 day fast. It really did make it a sacrifice now. I always looked forward to this camp meeting every year. Pass on or call it quits? I've come too far to turn back now.

I've met so many people from all walks of life. I enjoy people, you might think that I've not got too much to say, when in fact, I enjoy a good conversation because I like to hear different people's ideas and attitudes. I've learned that a smart person knows all the answers, but an intelligent person knows the right questions. I know what I know, but when I learn what you know, I have learned something that I didn't know before.

I could see that this fast wasn't just for me. Too many friends were looking toward me, hoping and praying for the best. I was doing what a lot of them wished they could do, but they could not. Health issues, work issues, age, sugar, etc. so many things that made a fast of 40 days only a dream to them. But I knew we all have different callings in our lives, and we need to be faithful to our calling.

I purposed in my heart to **Philippians 3:14** *I press toward the mark for the prize of the high calling of God in Christ Jesus.*

I decided to go for the 40 days. I also decided that the last 20 days would be just on water. I would know that I gave it my best.

Chapter 22   Fasting, Day 21 on

Your body shuts down. Your bowls don't have any food to process so they don't do anything. Your hearing starts to go away because you get so thin that the Eustachian tubes close on you. It is those narrow tubes that connects the space behind the eardrum (the middle ear) with the back of your throat. It is like trying to "pop" your eardrums and they just won't pop. So, it really gets hard to hear.

It is hard to talk because your voice box has less room to move in because your neck gets thin. You start to sound like your old grandmother.

Your shoes don't fit any more because all the different places where your body stores fat, you now began to use it up. It gets hard to walk because you're just walking on your bones. I could look down at my rib cage and watch my heartbeat through my ribs. My heart rate changed because it was working harder.

My thoughts and prayers were to people that were fighting cancer, which also felt bad, sick, weak and had to face each day once again, day after day. My weariness would stop once I would start eating again, but theirs would still be there each day. Someone who was sick in body, wondering if life would be better another day.

And what about those that have lost someone, and their hurt or suffering wasn't because of sickness in the body, but in the soul. Some things you just can't change. But one good meal would deliver me from my weakness. My prayers were to those people.

Proverbs 13:12 *Hope deferred maketh the heart sick: but when the desire cometh, it is a tree of life.*

Psalms 109:24 My *knees are weak through fasting; and my flesh faileth of fatness.*

How do you encourage someone in their time of need?

Psalms 121:1-2 *A Song of degrees. I will lift up mine eyes unto the hills, from whence cometh my help.*

My help cometh from the LORD, which made heaven and earth.

I would get up each morning and wash my face. To keep my spirit up each and every day was the goal. To wake up in the morning feeling refreshed, get cleaned up and with each step, realize that I didn't have as much strength, so you just pushed on. Praying was the best place to go.

Church wasn't just setting there and saying "Amen", I was playing the drums each and every night. When service was over, I was glad just to slip away and go to bed to catch up on the strength.

Mark 14:38 *Watch ye and pray, lest ye enter into temptation. The spirit truly is ready, but the flesh is weak.*

If someone was still saying that I wasn't fasting, why was I now a 6'6" person that only weighs 117 lbs.? It took a lot to just keep going. Some people would come up to me and say with such compassion, "you must be very tired". I know they meant well, but they just reminded me of what I was trying to overcome, and it would just drag me down. It made me think, what do I say to someone that is going through sickness, weakness or something that "drags them down"? When Paul was beaten and imprisoned, he finally had a chance to talk to Agrippa.

Acts 26:2 *"I think myself happy, king Agrippa, because I shall answer for myself this day before thee touching all the things whereof I am accused of the Jews:"*

He thought himself happy. **Proverbs 17:22** *A merry heart doeth good like a medicine: but a broken spirit drieth the bones.*

When I would be with a person who needed a friend, I would always try to have a merry heart. Some one might think that I wasn't "bearing their grief or their sorrow" but on the contrary, you do want to have compassion and lift up their load or burden.

As I was driving the 300 miles to the Campground, my van started to miss fire. It got worse and worse the closer that I got. I only had 20 or 30 more miles to go but it didn't sound like I would make it. I was leaving a trail of white smoke as I drove.

I just asked the Lord to get me there and I'll do what I could to fix it. Fasting really helps you to have compassion. As my motor made more noises and more smoke as I got closer, I got thinking about people that I would see driving some old clunker, smoke pouring out the back. Maybe a bunch of children in the back seat. It made me pray from a heart that wanted the Lord to bless them in their time of need.

I got to the campground, I was pretty sure that one of the pistons had cracked or something causing that one cylinder to miss and smoke so bad. I went to bed in the van and prayed knowing that I would have to take the engine apart in the morning and fix it during the 7-day convention.

The next morning came too soon. I got some tools together and started to take the head off. One spark plug was "gunked up" so I knew which cylinder was messed up. I took the 2 bolts off the valve cover and removed it and was getting ready to remove the parts so I could "pull the head" off the engine. I was not looking forward to this because the head probably weighed 60 pounds which was almost half of my weight.

I was only 117lbs at the time. My muscles were gone, my hearing was gone, my energy was gone except my strength in the Lord was great. He just gives you strength from somewhere.

As I looked on the valve train and was getting ready to loosen those bolts, I happened to notice one nut on one of the valve adjusters was loose. It was on the cylinder that was miss firing! One loose lock-nut! 25 cents! That was the problem. I got a new lock-nut that day, cleaned the spark plug, and started it up! That fixed it. Thank you, Jesus!

Psalms 46:1 *God is our refuge and strength, a very present help in trouble.*

Sammy and Sharon Estes where dear friends that lived near the campground. I asked Sharon if she would fix my first meal when I finished the fast. I asked her if she would fix me strawberry Jell-O with bananas in it and some soft scrambled eggs   But, three days before the end of the fast. Bro Hall asked me to start a camp meeting that was about 80 miles from Carbon Hill. A town called Red Bay in Alabama.   That meant that I would miss the strawberry Jell-O with bananas and soft scrambled eggs to end the fast. He didn't know what a sacrifice this would be.

Well, I got in my van and drove west to this little town. I had never been there before, so I didn't know anybody. This was pre-GPS days. When I got there, I found the street for the people that I was supposed to stay with. They were really nice. They showed me the room that they had for me and the towels to clean up with.

When I walked into the kitchen, I opened the refrigerator door, and there, on the shelf, was a pan of strawberry Jell-O with bananas in it! She told me when she went to the grocery store, she saw these bananas, she felt like she was supposed to buy them, so she bought them and a box of strawberry Jell-O. She said she hadn't fixed this in a long time, but it sounded good now! Praise God!

Matthew 6:8 *Be not ye therefore like unto them: for your Father knoweth what things ye have need of, before ye ask him.*

I preached the Saturday night service. The Spirit of the Lord was there, not because I was fasting, but because He is God! He is worthy of our Praise!

Sunday morning came. The 41st day. I had made it! As I sat down at the breakfast table, the dear sister scrambled the eggs with lots of milk to make them soft. I blessed the food and blessed the Lord. It was so good. It was also sad to be slaved back to knowing that two or three times a day, you would have to stop everything you are doing and take time to eat. Some people think our strength comes from food, and vitamins, and calories, and proteins, and fiber and such forth, but our strength comes from the Lord!

Oh, the strawberry Jell-O with bananas tasted SO GOOD! The orange juice was awesome!

That morning I preached the Sunday service. They had dinner on the grounds with services again at 2:30. I felt good. Good service. They had all kinds of food on the tables. Even though I hadn't eaten a big meal in well over a month, the food seemed like I could enjoy it with a little moderation. So, I had some mashed potatoes, some apple sauce. I felt OK, so I tried one piece of barbequed chicken.

As the afternoon service started with special singing, I was to be the main speaker. When it came my part, I sang a song and then started on the message. Well, I should have preached on the resurrection because the piece of chicken that I ate started to get resurrected! Oh my, it hurt!

My stomach hadn't had anything solid in it for so long, I couldn't take it. I really felt like the bird was flapping its wings. I had to turn the service over back to the group and find a place to lie down. I was better by the next morning, so I only had soft scrambled eggs.

There is a balance to how we perceive things, we can make subliminal statements trying to get people to admire us or exalt us. There is a proper balance that we should have in anything that we do for the Lord. It would be easy to state how this fast brought me "closer to the Lord". But at the same time, it would leave the impression that I have "arrived" at a place closer to the Lord than you. And that is not true.

Romans 12:1 *I beseech you therefore, brethren, by the mercies of God, that ye present your bodies a living sacrifice, holy, acceptable unto God, which is your reasonable service.*

The Lord can speak to us individually for us to do or say something. We can be obedient to that "leading" or go our own way.

1Samuel 15:22 *Behold, to obey is better than sacrifice,*

I have seen ministers exalt themselves to others by leaving the impression that since other people are not "full time" Pastors or Evangelists, that those people are a lesser person. Shame on that attitude!

Romans 12:3 *For I say, through the grace given unto me, to every man that is among you, not to think of himself more highly than he ought to think; but to think soberly, according as God hath dealt to every man the measure of faith.*

There are sacrifices that Christians make every day that temper our spirits and try our fortitude. We must press on and overcome each of these trials every day. And nobody knows these battles. Battles that make you want to quit or give up.

Jude 1:3 *Beloved, when I gave all diligence to write unto you of the common salvation, it was needful for me to write unto you, and exhort you that ye should earnestly contend for the faith which was once delivered unto the saints.*

I was thankful for the opportunity to go on this fast. There are many things that I learned. There were many sacrifices that I had to make to fulfill the desire to finish the fast. Being faithful each and every day, not quitting, not giving up, keeping up my spirit and applying my heart to every work done under the sun. That was the personal reward that I received in the fast.

Chapter 23   Life's Lessons – Stuff I've Learned

When your Right - Your Right:

You can't plan to learn some things. It just comes along when it wants to and lets you make the decision on how you are going to learn from it.

When I was in the percussion section of the Ball State University Orchestra. It was about 150 members strong. I played the tympani and Chimes. We did a beautiful rendition of "America the Beautiful." In the opening, there was a beautiful chime solo that just put the "kiss" on the music. It was to be as if there was a little Church out on the hillside that "chimed" the note to ring out across the country.

*"America, America, God shed his grace on thee. . . . ." **Ding** . . . .*

But, before the orchestra warms up, the leaders of each section goes down to the tuning machine and tunes his horn or instrument to the machine. Then the leader goes back to his section and all the other musicians "tune" their instrument to the section leader's horn.

Well, somebody had accidentally moved the dial on the tuning instrument, it was ¼ of a note too high. So, the whole orchestra was tuned "sharp".   But since they were all tuned together to the instrument, they all sounded perfect.

"Here we go, America the Beautiful from the top. Ready"

*"America, America, God shed his grace on thee....." **DONK***

It was so embarrassing. I was "flat" by a ¼ of a tone.

"OK, let's do it again! Everyone on their parts. From to top."

*"America, America, God shed his grace on thee. . . . ." **DONK***

There wasn't anything I could do. The chimes are tuned from the factory. They are always perfect for years and years. They never go wrong. The note "C" is always a perfect "C". Every note is perfect every day. I realized **THEY** were **ALL** wrong! I looked to our section leader and told him. They are all tuned sharp!

Back to the glaring look of the conductor. "Ok, let's all get our parts right. From the top again."

Sweat was now beading on my forehead, running down my face. I knew it would happen once again.

"America, America, God shed his grace on thee. . . . ." **DONK**

"Ok, let's get someone that can play the chimes." The whole orchestra gets quiet with a few stares at me. Looks of contempt, disbelief that a guy could not simply hit a chime right.

The percussion leader comes over to the chimes to take them from me. I quickly told him, "They are ALL tuned sharp." Sweat now begins to form on his brow. He knows I'm right.

"All right now, let's get it right. America the Beautiful, from the top."

"America, America, God shed his grace on thee. . . . ." **Doink . . . .**

The section leader barely pressed his knee against the chime so it wouldn't ring out hoping to cover up the sound of the "flat" chime.

I think the director realized that a chime can't be sharp or flat. It is always in perfect pitch. So, what is the lesson to be learned? Let's make this a multiple choice. You can pick just one or select them all because all answers are correct.

A. If you are right. It doesn't matter. You're right.

2. You can't change right to make it "righter".

D. Right or Wrong is not established by vote. Being solely right is better than being collectively wrong.

4. You can't make your right wrong just to "fit in". You can't take a hacksaw and cut off the bottom of the chime to make it "right". Because, just as soon as everyone tunes the next time, they will then be right, and you will still be "wrong" again in the eyes and ears of everyone. (Will he ever learn to play those chimes right?)

Matthew 7:13-14 *Enter ye in at the strait gate: for wide is the gate, and broad is the way, that leadeth to destruction, and many there be which go in thereat:*
Because strait is the gate, and narrow is the way, which leadeth unto life, and few there be that find it.

To some people, you are and will always be the person that doesn't know how to hit a pipe with a hammer to make the right sound. This gives them great relief that they are and always will be better than you. But to you, and you alone, you understand that your part in life, even though it is just one little Ding, it represents the finishing touch to the bigger picture.

Because, when all parts are put together, that little ding, was actually the "Angel of the Lord" that kissed that little bell on the little Church on the side of the hill that rang across the countryside.

"America, America, God shed his grace on thee." **Ding . . . . !**

Chapter 24   Life's Lessons – Sin will take you farther.

Sin will take you farther than you wanted to go.

I had a roommate, back in college, that worked at a restaurant that served tap beer and steamed hot dogs. The company policy was to empty whatever beer was left in the 21-gallon kegs each night and start with a fresh keg of beer each day. My roommate would take empty plastic gallon milk jugs each night and bring home the beer.   Let me say this, if you have free beer, you have a lot of friends.

One year we had a hog roast. It was out in a field in central Florida. There was a little Airstream trailer and benches all about. We cooked the pig over the fire for a long time getting ready for the roast. We then had this great bonfire for the evening.

I remember that there was a very pretty girl that came to the roast. She had a date with a fellow that just didn't "fit in".   He was obnoxious and after a few beers he got louder as the evening went on.

I remember her from the campus.   She had very long beautiful hair. She was always modestly dressed and had a wholesomeness about her that just didn't "fit in" with our crowd.   I can remember thinking to myself, "Why does she want to be with us?"

Of course, I had no idea of what a Christian was or what one looks like, but now looking back, I can see that she was a good Christian girl that hoped she could "fit in" with the "in crowd."

As the night went on, they were setting at the table in the tiny Airstream trailer drinking beer. That is when the oscillating fan caught her hair and wrapped it up into the fan blades. It tangled up her beautiful hair so bad that her drunk date took scissors and cut all her hair off.

That long beautiful hair now gone and leaving her with a scraggly crew cut. When classes resumed the next Monday, the laughter and gossip went across the campus. She got all her hair cut off by a drunk who didn't care.

I look back at this situation now and understand that this was a fine Christian girl that wanted to see if she could "be a part" of the worldly crowd.

2nd Corinthians 6:14 *Be ye not unequally yoked together with unbelievers: for what fellowship hath righteousness with unrighteousness? and what communion hath light with darkness?*

Chapter 25   Life's Lessons – Provoke good works.

We have an impact on people. We all have an effect on people.

There was a fellow in the youth group named Larry. Larry was the kind of fellow that wanted to do everything his own way. Have you noticed how that you can always see other people's flaws? Well I could see that no matter how something could be done, Larry would always want to do it his way.

One morning, we woke up to find everything covered with a thin sheet of ice. All the cars were covered, the trees, everything. It was beautiful, but we had to leave out for a Church Revival that morning.

Of course, all the windshields were covered with this coating of ice. The defrosters would do the job, but it would take a good bit of time. As I was scraping my windshield and doing my best to get down under the layer of ice, I noticed that Larry was going to take charge and show everyone how to get the "job done".

Larry was using a brick and tapping on the windshield to try and break up the ice. He always liked to do everything the "bold" way to get everything done. If you told him that there was a better way, he would be contrary and do it his way just to show you that he was the "boss".

Well, I had seen this in him, so as he was tapping on the windshield, I told him, "Larry, you'd better be careful."

I didn't tell him this because I cared, but because, in my heart, I knew that he would get belligerent and "show me how it's done." And sure enough, Larry tapped on the windshield ever harder until we heard the glass crack. TISCHE!

I knew that was going to happen, I had told him so. If he only would have listened to me, this wouldn't have happened.

74

But the problem was, I knew it would happen, especially if I would tell him to be careful, I knew that he would be provoked to try harder to prove "his" point.

See, I was right. Larry needed to be more careful. In my own smugness, I was the better person, Larry was just too rebellious for his own good. I knew that he didn't have enough money to get the windshield fixed. I knew that he would even have to save up money just to go find an old windshield from some junk yard.

Hebrews 10:24 *And let us consider one another to provoke unto love and to good works:*

The sad part of this whole story was that I really knew that I would provoke Larry to do the wrong thing if I said something, so I did.

We can affect what people do by what we say to them, and how we treat them.

I got the ice off the windshield of my van and that evening a bunch of us loaded up for the trip. The trip would take all night so we each took turns driving. It was now late in the night. I had been driving for several hours and I was ready to turn it over to someone else so I could get some sleep.

I pulled into a truck stop to take a break and change drivers. I always like to have a clean windshield, so I got out of the van to get the windshield clean for the next driver. I got a scrub brush from the dispenser at the gas pump and started shaking water onto the window to get ready to clean it.

Someone said, "Craig, you'd better be careful."

I know what I am doing, so I dipped the brush back in the bucket and started to shake the water on the window again even harder. Well, you guessed it, the brush slipped in my hand just enough for me to smack the windshield. TISCHE! The sound was unmistakable.

I had shattered my windshield.

Galatians 6:7 *Be not deceived; God is not mocked: for whatsoever a man soweth, that shall he also reap.*

I couldn't believe it, but I felt so relieved. I had been carrying the guilt of knowing that I provoked Larry that morning to cause him to shatter his windshield. And now it had come back around to me.

Matthew 7:2 *For with what judgment ye judge, ye shall be judged: and with what measure ye mete, it shall be measured to you again.*

It was someone else's turn to drive, so I went in the back of the van and laid down on the cot. I slept so well. The burden of guilt was gone. I slept.

About sunrise the next morning, we stopped to change drivers. We fueled up the van. I washed the window again. I felt so rested, so I took the next turn driving.

It was a beautiful morning. The sun was coming up. The cracked window in front of me. Life was good.

The van had a huge, one-piece windshield. But just the driver side was shattered. It made a big spider web look on the left side while the passenger side was untouched.

Everyone was now sleeping in back. The road had its familiar hum as the miles were clicking away. I began to think about what all had happened the night before. Joking with Larry, watching him break his windshield, then me smashing my windshield.

I was thinking to myself, "You know, that was just a coincidence, Larry breaking his windshield and me just breaking my windshield. It was just a coincidence."

I don't know why I thought it, everyone was asleep, but I then said out loud. "Yes, it was just a coincidence."

No sooner than I finished speaking, a crack started across the windshield. Within seconds, it made it across the complete windshield!

"Oh, dear Jesus!   Forgive me!   It was you!   It was you!   I know it was you!"

I got my windshield replaced a week or so later.   But nobody knows the lesson that I learned that day.

Hebrews 10:24 *And let us consider one another to provoke unto love and to good works:*

After Jesus had washed the disciple's feet, he shared a beautiful statement.

John 13:15 *For I have given you an example, that ye should do as I have done to you.*

Chapter 26   Life's Lessons - What are you looking at?

I enjoy riding a bicycle. I have a 20-year-old mountain bike and a 55+ year old road bicycle that was given to me by friends named the Reids from Arden, NC, after they bought it for $25 dollars at a yard sale. It doesn't matter how much you pay for a bicycle; you still have to supply the manpower to move the bike.

I live in a valley with 3,000-foot mountains on either side. There is a dirt road that crosses the mountain that I enjoy riding. It is 3 miles ride to the top and rises about 1,000 feet in the process. This is not what I call fun, it is what I call perseverance.

It takes about an hour of peddling to get to the top. There are rocks and ruts and all kinds of obstacles that you have to face each and every time. Nobody uses this road so if a tree or branch falls, it stays.

This may not seem like it is worthy of a "life lesson" but I discovered that you can always learn something each and every time you try something.

The only real "fun" in climbing this mountain, is the satisfaction of roaring down the mountain when you come back. But even this is not a fair trade off. Because it takes over an hour of hard sweaty pedaling to get to the top. I mean pedaling in the "granny gear" all the way to the top. In fact, you actually could go faster by walking the bike up beside you, than peddling all the way up in the "granny gears". So, after climbing and sweating for an hour, it only takes 15 minutes to coast off the mountain. Let's see: one hour of grunting for 15 minutes of screaming. Not a good trade, but I'll take it.

One problem that I always had was this one stone. After grunting away for an hour, there is this rock. It was only about 3 inches tall sticking up in the middle of the road at about 100 yards from the top. But when my front tire hit the rock, it would always bring me to a complete halt. It never failed. I would think about this rock as I neared the top. I had plenty of time the think and prepare myself for this rock. And as sure as I approached it, I was ready.

I knew how to do the "bunny hop", which is a trick where you pull up on the handlebars and peddles real hard causing both tires off the ground, but this never worked.

I knew how to do a wheel stand so that the front wheel would leave the ground and miss the rock, but this never worked.

It didn't matter what I tried, my front tire would hit this rock and I would come to a complete stop. . . . . .

One day I was talking with another mountain biker about this problem. His answer was "Don't look at the rock."

No really, what do I do to get over the rock?

He told me, "Don't look at the rock, look beside the rock."

I really did want to know what technical trick that I needed to do to get over the rock.

So, the next time that I got up to the top, I knew the rock was waiting for me, I looked right beside the rock, and guess what? My front tire missed the rock and I rode on as if it wasn't ever there.

Oh, come on!

You see it is a balance thing. You go where you are looking. If you are fixing your eyes on the rock, your balance will aim for that spot and your tire will follow your vision.

Ok, what is the message here?

What are you looking at?

Are you always looking to see if you can't pay the bills? Are you looking to see if you aren't smart enough to try something new? What are you looking at? That is where you are going.

Col_3:2 *Set your affection on things above, not on things on the earth.*

Don't set your goals based on what you see and limit yourself to what you think you can do. Look past your failure fixtures.

Hebrews 12:1 *Wherefore seeing we also are compassed about with so great a cloud of witnesses, let us lay aside every weight, and the sin which doth so easily beset us, and let us run with patience the race that is set before us,*

Hebrews 12:2 *Looking unto Jesus the author and finisher of our faith; who for the joy that was set before him endured the cross, despising the shame, and is set down at the right hand of the throne of God.*

Chapter 27   **Prayer: It is a place!**

My wife and I had moved to Virginia. We started a Computer Software Company that grew to serving 64 clients in 28 states. This one particular week was very slow. I didn't have any calls from companies for me to help with tech support, I didn't have any installations scheduled, so here it was the middle of the week and I didn't have any work lined up. I was thinking, "Lord, what are you going to do?".

I thought that I'd go to town and fuel up the car just in case somebody needs me. As I got to town and was pulling into a gas station, my cell phone rang. It was a client from Ohio calling because they had some computer server problem that the local guy couldn't solve. They wanted to know if I could come up and get the system up and running again.

I realized that they were 'down' and needed help fast. I told them that I would rearrange my schedule and get to them immediately. (OK, I didn't tell them the complete story.) I told them to get me a room for that night at the Hampton Inn and that I would be on the way within an hour. It would take me about 5 hours to drive so I should get there about 9:00pm and we could start work first thing in the morning.

After hanging up the phone, I realized that it was a blessing that I was available to them, and at the same time, the Lord had work for us to do.

Philippians 4:19 *But my God shall supply all your need according to his riches in glory by Christ Jesus.*

I didn't plan this trip, I didn't know about the trip, but God did. I decided to really dedicate this trip to Him in thanks.

I swung by the house and got my laptop and suitcase and took off for Ohio. I arrived at the motel about 8:30 that evening. I got checked in, unpacked my things and got ready to do some reading when I heard a loud commotion down the hall. It was bad! This was a nice motel, but there was a real problem down the hall. It didn't sound like a domestic problem, but it was well out of hand. I called the front desk and told them that there was a problem on my floor and not come check it out, but to call the police immediately.

Within minutes I saw the police go by the peep hole in my door. Whatever the problem was, they took someone with them when they left. I had no idea what happened, but I figured that it would be the conversation in the morning around the continental breakfast.

I didn't plan this trip, but God did. Since this was a last-minute trip, I purposed to do some praying in the hotel that night.

Psalms 100:4 *Enter into his gates with thanksgiving, and into his courts with praise: be thankful unto him, and bless his name.*

There is a time when we pray to give thanks before we eat or pray to start the day. These are short prayers for his blessings. Then there is a time of prayer that the Bible talks about called prayer and supplication.

Philippians 4:6 *Be careful for nothing; but in everything by prayer and supplication with thanksgiving let your requests be made known unto God.*

I remember reading when Abraham Lincoln was President, he made the statement, "I have been driven many times upon my knees by the overwhelming conviction that I had nowhere else to go."

Prayer is a place that you go to have fellowship with God. Being thankful to God opens the gate to prayer. *Enter into his gates with thanksgiving.* **Psalms 100.** I began to thank the Lord for all he has done in my life. I thanked him in prayer for all the times that I remembered seeing him move in my life.

Proverbs 3:6 *In all thy ways acknowledge him, and he shall direct thy paths.*

I had received the "Holy Ghost" years ago which is a gift that God gives his children, so I freely prayed and praised Him while praying in "tongues".

Romans 8:26 *Likewise the Spirit also helpeth our infirmities: for we know not what we should pray for as we ought: but the Spirit itself maketh intercession for us with groanings which cannot be uttered.*

1st Timothy 2:8 *I will therefore that men pray everywhere, lifting up holy hands, without wrath and doubting.*

To me, when you really enter into his courts with praise, it takes a while. You might think about this and about that, but the more you pray, the more these distractions sort of drop out of the way.

Jude 1:3 *Beloved, when I gave all diligence to write unto you of the common salvation, it was needful for me to write unto you, and exhort you that ye should earnestly contend for the faith which was once delivered unto the saints.*

You just keep praying until you reach that place that nothing else maters but this prayer that you are praying. To me, sometimes I walk the room praying. I might cry out to God and pour my soul out to him in tears. But the important thing is to press on in prayer.

Philippians 3:14 *I press toward the mark for the prize of the high calling of God in Christ Jesus.*

As I prayed on into the night, it was as if the Spirit of Prayer had lifted, I knew that I was through praying. I looked at the clock and it was now 3:00 AM in the morning. I was amazed because it only seemed that I had been praying for maybe an few minutes, when in fact, I had been praying for hours. I would still have time to get about 5 hours of sleep before I needed to go into the office. I was glad that I was given the time to pray and had the opportunity to pray.

I woke up about 8:00 AM and really felt rested and refreshed and ready to start the day. I went down for breakfast and wondered what happened down the hall that night. I was listening to hear if anyone was talking about the commotion that had happened, and sure enough, one lady was telling someone about something that happened. "There is no sense in that!"

I leaned over so I could hear more.

She was saying, "There is no sense in that, praying and crying like that, all night long!"

What? I couldn't believe it. Someone got assaulted and another arrested and this lady instead was more bothered by hearing someone praying?

Psalms 55:*17 Evening, and morning, and at noon, will I pray, and cry alound: and he shall hear my voice.*

Jude 1:17 *But, beloved, remember ye the words which were spoken before of the apostles of our Lord Jesus Christ;*
Jude 1:18 *How that they told you there should be mockers in the last time, who should walk after their own ungodly lusts.*
Jude 1:19 *These be they who separate themselves, sensual, having not the Spirit.*
Jude 1:20 *But ye, beloved, building up yourselves on your most holy faith, praying in the Holy Ghost,*
Jude 1:21 *Keep yourselves in the love of God, looking for the mercy of our Lord Jesus Christ unto eternal life.*

Chapter 28   A word fitly spoken

Proverbs 25:11 *A word fitly spoken is like apples of gold in pictures of silver.*

Sometimes a word or a thought comes into mind that you didn't even have any thought on. Usually it will be something encouraging.

Several of the other guys from Cleveland set a gospel tent up in Orlando, Florida. The youth group was there and reaching out to people on the street. The tent was set on the "Orange Blossom Trail" which was the "street walkers" area of town. I arrived in the evening, the services were already in progress and people were praying all around the tent. Some in the altar area and others were standing or sitting around the back of the tent.

There was one young lady standing in the row of chairs in front of me, so as I thought she was praying, I leaned over to her and said what was on my heart. I said to her "I will make you as pure as wind driven snow".

She stepped out of the row where she was standing and went down to the altar area of the tent. I went around to others to see who wanted prayer. All and all, it was a good service that night and many people were getting a blessing.

Isaiah 1:18 *Come now, and let us reason together, saith the LORD: though your sins be as scarlet, **they shall be as white as snow;** though they be red like crimson, they shall be as wool.*

As the service was "coming to a close", the speaker asked if anyone wanted to share or testify. The young lady came forward that I saw in the back and spoke a word to. She began to tell the people this,

"You all know me. I work this section of the street. I heard the singing and saw you all here. I know what you feel. I used to have what you all have. But I was so far away from God. I didn't even know if God would hear me. My life was such a mess." She said that she bowed her head and asked God if he could forgive her. She then said that she heard a voice say, "I'll make you as pure as wind driven snow."

That was when she went down to the altar.

This young lady went with us after the services each night and we spoke to dozens of gals that needed to hear the mercy of Jesus. It was tough, they had heard so much from so many, that it was hard to let them know that you were telling the truth with no other motive except for them to be saved. It was also sad to hear that many of these gals had known the Lord early in their life, things happened, and they made the wrong choices and here is where they ended up.

Later, one night that week, a red Cadillac with a white landau top, with all the chrome changed to Brass, pulled up and stopped. In the street lit night, I saw the driver raise a chrome plated gun and he pointed it at me.

Is this IT? My life ends like this? There was no place to hide, run or duck. This is IT! Just as quickly as this was happening, all the girls ran around me and hid me in their crowd. They yelled at the guy "Leave him alone, he's with us!"

He drove on, and it was a comfort to know that I had won the confidence of the girls. Several of them continued coming to the tent revival and I hope the Lord is still working in their lives.

1 Corinthians 10:13 *There hath no temptation taken you but such as is common to man: but God is faithful, who will not suffer you to be tempted above that ye are able; but will with the temptation also make a way to escape, that ye may be able to bear it.*

It is easy to want to fill a Church with fine Christian people. Bible believing, hair combed, pressed pants and singing every song that you like to hear. But Jesus went out to the hedges and highways to find those that had need of him.

Matthew 9:12 *But when Jesus heard that, he said unto them, They that be whole need not a physician, but they that are sick.*

Matthew 9:13 *But go ye and learn what that meaneth, I will have* **mercy**, *and not* **sacrifice**: *for I am not come to call the righteous, but sinners to repentance.*

Jesus picked a simple fisherman named Peter and taught him to become fishers of men.

He can take an educated man, named Saul, who hated what Christians stood for. Hated them so much that he caused Christians to be put to death. This man was blinded by God so that he could see clearly later. He went on the write the majority of the New Testament in the Bible. He was named Saul, but God gave him a new life and a new name, Paul.

He can take a woman of Samaria who was a five-time failure in marriages. In fact, the one she was with now, was number six and he wasn't even hers. But this next man she met at the well told her everything that she did. The city that shunned her because of her life, gladly received her when she told them that a man named Jesus changed her life,

Jesus can a take crippled man from birth and cause him to walk.

Jesus can take a blind man and cause him to see.

Jesus can take a woman sick for 12 years, who had spent all of her money going to every doctor that couldn't find the cure to being instantly healed by just touching the hem of Jesus' garment. Known as the woman with the issue of blood.

Jesus can take a dead man to hear Jesus' spoken word to come back to life. His name is Lazarus.

Jesus can take a young boy who cut himself and threw himself against the rocks and walls to a boy that is completely sane and in his right mind.

Philippians 2:10 *That at the name of Jesus every knee should bow, of things in heaven, and things in earth, and things under the*

earth;

Philippians 2:11 *And that every tongue should confess that Jesus Christ is Lord, to the glory of God the Father.*

Chapter 29   The Prodigal Son

It was a tent meeting outside of Chattanooga Tennessee A lot of local people were coming to the tent. I saw a young man in his early 20's, standing outside the tent. His hair was down past his shoulders. He was listening but wasn't getting into the service. So, I made my way back to him to talk. He seemed like a good guy, just carrying a lot of problems. I talked with him a while and then suggested that we go up to the altar and pray. Prayer couldn't hurt, maybe God would really help.

So, he went to the altar and began to pray. It was great. He really prayed. Nothing like watching someone open their heart to the Lord and really pray.

1st Peter 5:6 *Humble yourselves therefore under the mighty hand of God, that he may exalt you in due time*:
1st Peter 5:7 Casting *all your care upon him; for he careth for you.*

After service, I asked him if there was anything I could do to help. He said that he had to change some things. He got saved that night and he knew that he had to follow them up. He was living with his girlfriend and they were not married. He told me that he knew it was not right. So, we hopped in my van and went to the house.

I got to tell you. When you are forgiven, you know when it happens, and you know that you will not be the same. On the way over to the house, he was just overjoyed.

It was now about 11:30 pm or so when we went into the house, his girlfriend was there and was wondering what had happened. I don't remember her name, but what he said was something like this. "Becky! Look, it's me!"

She looked at me like, "Ok, what is he on now?" He told her that he couldn't live here anymore that the "Lord saved him". He started to gather his things.

I told her that he went to a tent revival and got "Saved". I told her to give him some time. Things will work out.

You know, you don't "get saved" to run from responsibility. You don't get saved to keep the IRS off your back or get you out of debt, or make sure you don't flunk a test. You get saved because you are a sinner.

Romans 6:23 *For the wages of sin is death; but the gift of God is eternal life through Jesus Christ our Lord.*

I truly believe that this young man made the right decision for all the right reasons, but this young woman had her hopes dashed because her "live in" got "saved". God cared for the soul of that young woman as much as her boyfriend.

I assured her that she needed to be patient with the situation, and let the Lord work it out. I told her that his life was going to change, and it would be to the good.

He packed up his stuff and then told his girlfriend that he wanted to go see his dad. He even asked that we all prayed here together before he left. I know it was a bit much for the girlfriend, but this was what was going to happen. So, we prayed together and then left.

It was neat. The guy's heart was so changed on the inside, that he even thought that he looked different on the outside.

It was now getting midnight, or thereabout, and going up to the steps of his dad's house was going a little farther that I was planning on that night. There were no lights on, it was dark, I didn't even know how I was going to find my way back. (pre-GPS).

So, he knocked on the door, a light came on in the back, and the door opened.

The man had been sleeping, his son walked up to his dad and told him that he got right with the Lord. It was amazing! His dad was a Minister and his son had come home!

Oh man! I have read about the prodigal son, but here it was in action. The father put his arms around his son and began to weep and praise God! His dad reached out and included me in this hug. His wayward son had come home!

It was great! Seeing a New Testament scripture come to life. We talked for a while, it was as if I was an old friend of the family, but in fact, we were all now part of God's family.

Luke 15:*10 Likewise, I say unto you, there is joy in the presence of the angels of God over one sinner that repenteth.*
Luke 15:11 *And he said, A certain man had two sons:*
Luke 15:12 *And the younger of them said to his father, Father, give me the portion of goods that falleth to me. And he divided unto them his living.*
Luke 15:13 *And not many days after the younger son gathered all together, and took his journey into a far country, and there wasted his substance with riotous living.*
Luke 15:14 *And when he had spent all, there arose a mighty famine in that land; and he began to be in want.*
Luke 15:*15 And he went and joined himself to a citizen of that country; and he sent him into his fields to feed swine.*
Luke 15:16 *And he would fain have filled his belly with the husks that the swine did eat: and no man gave unto him.*
Luke 15:*17 And when he came to himself, he said, How many hired servants of my father's have bread enough and to spare, and I perish with hunger!*
Luke 15:18 *I will arise and go to my father, and will say unto him, Father, I have sinned against heaven, and before thee,*
Luke 15:19 *And am no more worthy to be called thy son: make me as one of thy hired servants.*

Luke 15:20 *And he arose, and came to his father. But when he was yet a great way off, his father saw him, and had compassion, and ran, and fell on his neck, and kissed him.*

Luke 15:21 *And the son said unto him, Father, I have sinned against heaven, and in thy sight, and am no more worthy to be called thy son.*

Luke 15:22 *But the father said to his servants, Bring forth the best robe, and put it on him; and put a ring on his hand, and shoes on his feet:*

Luke 15:23 *And bring hither the fatted calf, and kill it; and let us eat, and be merry:*

Luke 15:24 *For this my son was dead, and is alive again; he was lost, and is found. And they began to be merry.*

Chapter 30   **A rushing mighty wind.**

I stayed one weekend with a good friend of mine, Robert Elswick and his wife Patty. I was ministering in the Church that they were attending on the Sunday morning. We had dinner after Church and then that afternoon, went to a Baptizing. It was a fall day, beautiful clear sky, perfect for an outdoor Baptismal service.

I had scheduled a service for that evening about 40 miles from where the Baptism was being held, but I went to the Baptism with Robert and Patty. The minister wanted it to be a memorable service, so he was praising God and Speaking in Tongues and shivering all at the same time in the water. I kind of thought it was more cold water than the "Spirit", but whatever. He baptized several and it was nice, but I really did have to get going to be at the other Church that evening.

I turned to Patty and said, "Well, better go."

Patty turned and looked at me for a moment. She handed her purse to her husband, took her shoes off and started to the water.

I thought, "No, I mean that I'd better go!" But she was on her way.

Robert and Patty lived way out on a road nearly 15 miles out of town. There were only a few homes that you passed on the way to their home. So, Patty was known to really pray a prayer through.

Robert, Patty, my wife Linda and I had a real friendship. They were known in the County as Buster and Patty. They were quite wealthy as Buster owned a coal mine that was quite successful at the age of 30. When hunting season came, Buster would close the mine down and take all the miners hunting big game in Canada.

People hung around Buster and Patty, hoping that they would get something from the Elswick. Buster and Patty knew that and that's why we became good friends. We didn't want anything from them except their love and friendship.

As Patty went down to the water, she wanted to be baptized in the Name of Jesus. As the minister lowered her into the water, a rush of wind blew through the trees above the ridge above the little branch of water. As he rose Patty up from the water, all these fall leaves gently floated down and landed in the water all around her. It was amazing! All I could say was, "like a rushing mighty wind".

Latter we talked about the service. She had not been baptized in the Name of Jesus before. She had read the scriptures concerning Baptism and saw that all the Baptisms in the New Testament were "In the Name of Jesus". She said that she felt the Spirit of the Lord was leading her to go and be baptized that day but didn't know what the people would think.
About that time, I said, "Well, better go."

One day, Robert and I were flying around in his Cessna 182. He pointed to a mountain that we were flying by and he said, "That mountain will kill somebody someday." Little did he know that it would come to pass that he would be the one that would be killed in a plane crash on that mountain. The family asked me to preach his funeral. I did my best I could to share who Robert really was.

Patty passed away several years' latter.

Chapter 31   God, it's your call.

However you want this to go.

My wife, Linda, had gone to Kentucky for the weekend to attend a great niece's baby shower. That was fine with me because there were a lot of things that I wanted to get done around the house while she was gone.

I needed to replace an old fuel line on our 30-year-old Cub Cadet lawn tractor so this Friday night would be the perfect time. I had shut off the fuel supply at the bottom of the gas tank and situated myself sitting with my legs under the tractor so I could get to the old fuel line with my right hand. I was holding the shop light with my left hand so I could see better. The light had the old style 60-watt bulb that put off a lot of heat and you could also plug in another cord in the outlet.

I was pulling on the fuel line to remove it from the shutoff valve when the whole valve popped off the gas tank. Fuel began flowing out of the tank, soaking my legs and arms with gasoline. I could reach the hole, but the hole was bigger than my fingers could plug up. The pool of gasoline was now spreading out across the carport and flowed underneath both our cars. There were still more gallons of gas in the tank to spill out. I could get my thumb to cover the hole, but now I realized the terrible situation that I was in. My left hand was holding the ignition source, the hot trouble light. I couldn't take my right hand off the hole, but I had to get rid of the light. So, I tossed the light as hard as I could out into the back yard.

As I sat in the pool of gasoline, I realized how bad a situation that I was in. If the gas would find another ignition source, it would be a consuming fire that I could not run from. Covered with gas, it would be terrible burns, if not fatal for me. The gas, now covering the carport, would set the house on fire and living in the country, would take too much time for someone to see the fire, call for help and help arrive. I was setting in God's mercy. I thought, "God, it's your call. However, you want this to go."

It is amazing how many thoughts go through your heart when you are in a crisis. You think about family and loved ones and hope that they will understand. You hope they don't worry about if you suffered or whatever. But you just realize that your life is in God's hands and his mercy.

I still had more gas to spill out of the tank. I saw an empty 40 lb. plastic bag for water softener salt within reach of my left hand. I got it under the tank and removed my thumb. The bag filled up about halfway before the tank ran out. I got out from under the tractor and got the garden hose to spray the gas off the carport. I knew that the water would only spread the gas out more, so the threat of fire was even greater, and my clothes were still soaked with gas. I finally got the gas washed off the carport and away from the house.

Life can change so quickly. One event can change everything. I believe that this is the first time that I thanked the Lord for what didn't happen. We always thank Him for He does in our lives, but do we thank Him for what He protects us from. This coming year, I see the importance of praying, *"Not my will, but Thy will be done."*

Chapter 32   **Wrong Number**

Sometimes the blessing works in the opposite direction. God knows your needs; he knows when you are at your end.

I knew a pastor friend in Alabama, Bro Larry & Martha Perkins, that told me to call him sometime to arrange to minister in his Church. I had the number in my wallet and knew that someday I would. Well maybe a year later I came across the number and remembered that I promised him that I would call.

So, I dialed the number and his wife answered. I said, "Is Larry there?"

She said "No he isn't"

I could tell that there was a distance in her answer, so I asked if I should call back later.

She said he is not here anymore but is living with his mother.

I hated to hear that because they were good people. They had a good Church and a good marriage. I went on to tell her that the Lord knows the situation and somehow, he will work it out for you. I could hear the sister crying on the other end. Sometimes we need to know that God knows what we are going through. I told her that I would keep them both in prayer.

I asked her, "What about Church? Are you both still going?" It got kind of quiet on that end, I knew it might be embarrassing to her. "Is he still pastoring the Church?"

She said "No, he's not a pastor."

I said. "Is this Bro. Perkin's wife?"

She said "No, this is (her name)!"

The number I dialed was the WRONG NUMBER!

I don't know who it was on the other side of the line, but God knew, and He helped me dial the number to tell her that He was there for her!

Psalms 46:1 God is *our refuge and strength, a very present help in trouble.*

What started out to me was a conversation with an old friend, ended up with sharing the Lord and His comfort to a person that really needed some help. God knows every situation that we are facing. He is a very present help in trouble.

Chapter 33   Opportunity

I was out in Texas on a business trip. I drove instead of flying out because I had several companies to visit on this trip. So, I worked my way out to clients in Arkansas, Oklahoma, then down to Texas, and finally down to Louisiana and on back to home. As I was leaving St Charles, La, this one morning, it dawned on me that I would be going through Baton Rouge, Louisiana.

I had an old friend, Pat Hayes, who was the assistant pastor of a Church in Baton Rouge. Brother Pat was my best man at our wedding, and it had been nearly 15 years since we had seen one another. What a great way to surprise him.

Years before, Pat would set an old Gospel Tent in a town and have a youth group reach out to the community with personal witnessing and then have services in the evening. A lot of good works came from this outreach. Whenever Pat set the tent, I would try to be there to help set it up.

So, this day, as I drove into Baton Rouge, I thought that I would look up Brother Pat. I stopped at a phone booth (this is before cell phones were invented) and looked up Pat's name. Sure enough, there it was. I called the number and his wife answered. She was pleasantly surprised. Pat wasn't home but was at the Church. In fact, Pat was setting a tent at the Church so that the youth group could have special services. I told his wife not to let Pat know that I was in town, but to give me directions to the Church.

Now Pat was setting the tent with the help of the Church's young men. They had been working hard in the hot sun putting up poles, raising the tent and driving in the tent stakes. They had built a platform for the music and the podium and were finishing putting chairs up in the tent.

They had stopped to take a break. Pat was telling the young men about a friend of his, named Craig Strain, that was always there whenever he set a tent. They were all interested as Pat was reminiscing of the things that we had done together for the work of the Lord. No doubt that it was intriguing to these young men as they heard these stories.

About that time, I drove up!

The young men walked up to the car as if I was some walking legend that they were going to talk with and stand next to. I got out and sat down under the tent with them. They were amazed how this all came to pass. Just as Pat was talking about this Christian friend, I drove up.

Galations 6:10 *As we have therefore* **opportunity**, *let us do good unto all men, especially unto them who are of the household of faith.*

If there is a lession from this, I say it is because of the one word, opportunity. How many times in your life do you think about doing something, visiting someone or going someplace, or calling someone and you choose not to do it?

As I left the motel early that morning, I remembered that, last I knew, Pat was in Baton Rouge. Of course, as I thought about looking up Pat, I thought he might not be home, or he has moved, or I don't have the time. All kinds of thoughts that would keep me from just trying to see if Pat was there. I wouldn't be in Louisiana for another year or two, so why not stop, why not try, why not take the time. Here is the **opportunity**. How many times do you see in your life that you could take the opportunity to take the time to see if God is in it?

What ended up as a great time to fellowship with an old friend, turned out to be a blessing from the Lord to these young Christians, who saw how God performed this miracle of sorts. Pat was talking about this old friend and Poof! Here he is!

Step out in faith, test the opportunity that the Lord will place before you.

John 10:10 *The thief cometh not, but for to steal, and to kill, and to destroy: I am come that they might have life, and that they might have it more abundantly.*

Chapter 34   Late one night

Late one night as I was returning back to Cleveland Tennessee from a revival up in West Virginia, I stopped at a gas station to fill up. My van was a 1966 Chevrolet, it was old by this point, but it got me where I needed to go. A young longhaired man came out to my van and began talking to me saying, "Wow, what a cool Van!"

My van really wasn't that cool, but it was late at night so he couldn't see really how junky it was. So, I thought, "well maybe he's got a van he wants to talk about.", so I ask, "Do you have a van?" He said he did, but he was in a real bad wreak and totaled it. He had gone through the windshield and needed 200 stitches for his head.

We went into the gas station so I could pay the bill, and there was a bunch of other longhaired young men in the station. So, as I was getting ready to leave, I said to the fellow that was in the wreck, "You must have had someone praying for you to live."

The young man got quiet and said, "Yes, my Mom is a praying Mom." I asked the young man if he came out OK from the wreck. He said, "I can't straighten my leg. My knee doesn't work like it should."

So, I told him, "Well, let's just pray and see what God will do."

I knelt down to pray and put my hands on his knee. It really dawned on me, "What in the world are you doing, Craig?" I hadn't felt the leading of the Lord to pray, I just talked and here I am on my knees, praying in a gas station with all these guys standing around watching. What in the world am I going to do?

So, I started to pray, "Lord, touch this brother's knee, and heal him, in the name of Jesus." Then as I was going to really punch a hole in the sky with prayer, I felt the Spirit of the Lord for me to get up. Boy was I glad to know that he had been watching! So, I asked the young man to move his leg, and he was able to straighten it and bend it and straighten it and bend it!

All of us in the room just stood there in shock. We all started shaking hands and hugging one another. We knew we really saw God heal, in a gas station, in the middle of the night. As I shook hands with each of the guys, one of them jerked his hand away from me, and by his expression, you could see he didn't like this at all. I don't know if he was the ringleader of this group and didn't like this, or whatever his problem was, I knew he saw something very real.

Psalms 48:2 *Beautiful for situation, the joy of the whole earth, is mount Zion, on the sides of the north, the city of the great King.*

Chapter 35 Get a Vision

The desire that I have for each and every Christian, is to have a relationship with Jesus. To have a personal walk with the Lord in such way that a sinner can see that you have something life changing to offer them.

Acts 4:13 Now *when they saw the boldness of Peter and John, and perceived that they were unlearned and ignorant men, they marvelled; and they took knowledge of them, that they had been with Jesus.*

I believe that many of our Churches have moved from leading people to Jesus, to just entertaining the believers.

I spoke with a Police Officer that told me he worked with an individual that really needed help with a personal problem. He offered to take this person to a Church if they would be willing to go. The person agreed. The officer took them to a "Spirit filled Community Church" that looked like a good place to attend. When they got to the service, the lights went out, the spotlights and light show turned on, the singers (worship team) started their performance, and the band struck up. The Officer told me it was terrible.

After Church, the person that needed the help, said that they loved it. She didn't need to go to night clubs, the Church was "cooler" than the night clubs that she would go to.

Church isn't to entertain us. It is to ordain us. It is to redeem us from sin.

Proverbs_16:25 *There is a way that seemeth right unto a man, but the end thereof are the ways of death.*

Our goal should be to lead a sinner to Jesus who knows what they have need of. It is to reach for the lost.

Joh 21:15 *So when they had dined, Jesus saith to Simon Peter, Simon, son of Jonas, lovest thou me more than these? He saith unto him, Yea, Lord; thou knowest that I love thee. He saith unto him, Feed my lambs.*

Our goal shouldn't be to look down our noses to a person that has got caught up in sin, but to lead that person to one that will satisfy their soul.

Our goal isn't to show a person of how "close to God" that we are, but to show them how to receive God's grace and mercy as we have.

Philippians 4:17 Not *because I desire a gift: but I desire fruit that may abound to your account.*

Over the years I have watched people try to become "successful" in a ministry. Thinking that "if" they had a Church to pastor, "if" they were an evangelist, "if" they were a famous singer. It is a trap that pulls you away from the caring of your heart for a soul.

Our true "goal" should be to tell people who have tried everything except the Lord about His loving mercy and forgiveness. God can take care of your situation anytime you pray.

One day I was in Eola Park in downtown Orlando. A lot of transits and homeless gather on the street in that area. I remember taking a whole day witnessing to so many different people. I hadn't had anyone to ask for prayer. I just felt like I had just become a part of this whole "scene" of homeless, street people.

To be truthful, I believe that I really wanted something to happen so that I could share it with the Church that night, the "great thing" that I did that day. You know, "out witnessing for the Lord."

I've heard Churches brag about the number of people that they baptized in a service. The individual just becomes a number. "Guess how many we baptized today?" "How many people attend your Church?" "See how many cars are in our parking lot!"

See, it is so easy to lose sight of the soul of a sinner for the success of the Service.

So, as the day was "coming to a close", I was disappointed that I hadn't "won a soul" to the Lord. "I" had nothing to show for my work. IF you can hear what I am saying, it was all about me! Not about caring for a lost soul.

So, as I was walking back to the van, I saw this dumpster over behind this Convenience Store. I felt the Lord speak to my heart to go over to the dumpster. I was thinking, "Oh, come on Lord, this had not been a good day. I don't need to go dumpster diving."

But I went over to the dumpster anyway. As I looked in, there was a person, scavenging for some food. The reality for a person's needs really hit me. He wasn't a person that I could "win" to the Lord, he was a person that really needed to be blessed of God. We took some time to talk with one another and I slowly led the conversation to sharing the Gospel with this person. We ended in prayer, him asking to be forgiven of his sin, and me asking the Lord to forgive me of my desire to just "win a soul" instead of caring for a soul.

Chapter 36 Missions

America is so blessed. We have access to anything. All the comforts of home. See the world without ever leaving your comfortable chair. Go to the fridge and get what you want. You can even turn a faucet and have hot water.

You can hop into your car and go to Church. But here is the question, how many times during the week do you go to Church and for how long? I don't say this as a condemnation, but as a truthful statement.

No better way to state the difference in our choices of life, than when our group, Caribbean Missions led by Bro Tommy Ramsey, traveled all morning out across the dry grassy highlands of northwest Haiti. We arrived at a makeshift Church, built with four corner posts connected with branches and the roof was just a covering of grass and bushes. I am 6'6" tall and the roof was only about 6 feet tall. I had to stay bent over to preach the service that day. But the brush arbor was full of people that came because they heard missionaries were coming.

They had begun assembling early morning, singing, testifying, preaching and having "Church" until we arrived. We didn't get there until late afternoon. I say late afternoon because if I said 4:00 o'clock, that wouldn't matter to these people because didn't have clocks. You enter into a world that is totally different. It doesn't have rock stars, it doesn't have basketball stars, they don't have TVs or radios or internet because they don't even have electricity.

Later that day, we went on to another Church that we would be ministering at in that part of the country.. Our group had sent down a 2500-watt Electric Generator with a roll of wire and some "pig tails" (things you screw light bulbs into) to this Church that we had helped build. When they first turned on the motor, the circuit breaker popped. My brother-in-law, Robert Combs, and I followed the wire from pig tail to pig tail and didn't find anything wrong. But at the end of the wire, we found that they had stripped the ends and joined the two wires together. That is what caused the "short".

Now you and I know that you don't touch those wires together, but when you have never entered the world of electricity, how would you know? If you have never worked with computers, do you know how to ping an IP address? If you have never learned to sew, do you know about a seam allowance? It is not because of ignorance; it is because you've not been introduced into that world.

I told our interpreter that "Here is the problem, these wires cannot touch."

The interpreter immediately told me, "No, No. The electricity will spill out on the end."

After we taped the ends separately and turned on the generator, then he "saw the light". But even then, the lights were very dim, and the generator was struggling. I realized that he had too many lights connected, and the generator was lugging down. I told the interpreter that we need to turn off all the lights outside the Church so it will be brighter inside.

He told me, "No, no! We have lights, so we let our light so shine before men."

He was right. We hadn't seen a power pole for hours. The nearest light might be 60 or 70 miles away. This light was a "beacon" to all the surrounding mountains. We were a "city set on a hill."

We have an idea that when we give money to a Church organization's mission fund, that a great missionary work is put into action. But if you think about it, the organization has overhead, it has people, staff and many other expenses that use up the money. How much really goes to the missionaries and the people that you are helping?

No better example of this problem than when I had watched a nationally famous TV Evangelist show video of his "great outreach" with thousands of people in attendance. I had watched his weekly "show" and listened to his request for offerings to help these people.

When we were in the city in Port-a-Prince, Haiti, where this outreach was located, I asked our interpreter where these services were held. He looked at me and said, "They only come and put up signs to get a crowd. Then they leave. They do nothing for the people."

1 Thessalonians 5:12 And *we beseech you, brethren, to know them which labour among you, and are over you in the Lord, and admonish you;*

Chapter 37   **Everyone has Talents**

Where do you stop when you mention the names of people that you labor with in the Gospel? I don't even know the name of the man in the nursing home that was missing his leg. But there will be a day that I will see him again.

Bro Tommy Ramsey, who founded Caribbean Missions, opened up his mission trips to encourage others to have a chance at doing Mission work. People like Donnie and Pat Allen, David and Patty Crowell, Teresa Akers, Jewel and Jerry Williams and their daughter Lori, Robert Combs, Lucy French, Delane Repass, Vonda Lamie, Albert Woodyard, and of course, Linda and I and many others.

Each person brought their blessings to the people that came out to hear the Gospel. But each person brought something that the other person could not. They brought themselves. No one can be you.

Jeremiah 1:5 *Before I formed thee in the belly I knew thee; and before thou camest forth out of the womb I sanctified thee, and I ordained thee a prophet unto the nations.*

You never know how God can use you and the talents that he gave you. But God does.

We had been traveling for several hours in Haiti. The road had been reduced down to just a rough rocky road going across a desert. The average gravel road in the United States would look like a superhighway compared to this road. And this was the main road to travel up and down the coast of Haiti. Several times we came upon a person that had taken some small rocks and filled in a pothole. They would stand there all day until someone drove by. They would hold out their hand hoping you would pay them for fixing that hole in the road. Even though this was the main road, less than a handful of cars or trucks would ever pass by each day.

We were far from any town when our vehicle rolled to a stop. The engine just wouldn't pull the van any further. It ran out of power and it began to overheat and just stopped dead.

As far as the eye could see there was just nothing. Absolutely nothing!

Robert Combs was on this trip. He just wanted to come and serve the Lord on this mission trip.

Words don't describe how desolate you feel when you break down on a desolate road in a desolate country with no tools and no idea of what you are going to do. No need to worry about being broke down in the middle of the road because it might be tomorrow before the next vehicle comes by.

When I say truck comes by, you can hear it groaning for miles. It would be loaded down so heavy that it would make any DOT officer in America smile. The truck would be stacked with as much stuff as it could possibly carry and then add all the people that would be sitting on the truck, on its' roof, on the fenders, on the running boards, just everywhere a person could ride (along with their chickens) there would be riders. This was the main transportation to and from Port-a-Prince.

Robert had no tools, but he now knew why he was on this trip and what he needed to do. He checked. There was fuel going to the engine, there was electricity going to the sparkplugs, there was water in the radiator, and oil in the engine. But why is the engine dying?

111

Robert, from a kid, loved to take things apart. But more important than that, he knew how to put things back together. This was his calling. This breakdown was his challenge. Why are we dead in the road and how do we fix it?

He disappeared under the Van and after some banging and lots of noise making, Robert said it was fixed.

No tools? No wrenches? What did you do?

Robert realized that the van had been run on cheap leaded gas for years and that this van had a catalytic converter that was clogged up because of the leaded gas. Robert took a big rock and knocked off the tailpipe, muffler, and catalytic converter and we were ready to go.

Now we sounded like a true Haitian truck loaded down with our mission team singing to the top of our lungs to drown out the noisy van.

Life is good!

Chapter 38   People

You can't judge a book by looking at the cover. So it is with people.

We had been traveling for most of the morning in Haiti. It had been hours since we had even seen a power pole on the side of the road. The further we traveled, the more remote the area became.

The only homes that we saw were no more than just a house made with bamboo walls and a grass roof. Out behind the one room homes would be a kitchen made up with a cooking pot on a stand that would have a little bit of charcoal underneath to heat the food.

Every once in a while, we would see a mud home. This was actually a grass hut, but they had packed mud on the outside. This was a wealthier family. If they were upper middle-class people, there would be a door on the mud house.

As we entered into a little village, we stopped at the community Centre for some directions. Most of the buildings in the village were made of blocks or mud huts. In front of this one home was a man sweeping the yard in straight lines with a homemade broom. Think of this, he was sweeping the dust in straight lines. I thought this was kind of useless because it was just dust and dirt. But then I realized that when we are home, we mow the grass in straight lines. It looks nicer that way.

It showed to me that this person wasn't slothful or lazy. He wanted his "yard" to look nice. He had pride in what he owned. It made me realize that even though the culture was different, the diligence of the person was the same.

We arrived at the Church where we would be staying that week. We had some tasks that we wanted to accomplish during the week. One was to build a latrine. People had no place to go to the bathroom.

When a person needed to "go" they would just go. The women wear skirts, so they would squat down and arrange their skirt to maintain their modesty and do their job. Their culture allowed this, and nobody thought anything about it. It was just a fact of life. Add to this that the sun was so hot and baked everything, whatever moisture there was, it was dried up in a matter of minutes. We understood the uncleanness of this practice and planned to build a latrine for the community.

The hole had been dug and the block walls had been laid. We were building the roof on the latrine. One of the Haitians had a hammer and kept his nails in his hair. Every time he needed a nail, he pulled it out of his "head".

So, the next day, we were passing through a village. There was a general store that had some hardware. I bought a nail apron, a pound of nails, a hammer, a handsaw, a trowel and a plumb bob with some string. All in all, it cost me about 20 dollars American.

That evening, I ask the interpreter to get the man who was helping build the latrine to join us. When he arrived, I gave him the tools. These people are a proud and hardworking people, but he could not hold back tears of thankfulness. It was the best $20 I had ever spent.

The next morning, our interpreter asked me to come outside. He had someone that wanted to speak to me. The man that I had given the tools to the night before; he now had three other men standing with him that he had hired to work for him. One to cut wood with the saw, another to do the hammering, and the other to do the block work with the trowel and plumb bob. He now had a "construction company" and he was going out to find work for his crew to do.

I might as well have bought him a dump truck with a backhoe. He could have kept the tools for himself, but he thought of a better plan to help others. They all now had a job and a hope for a good future.

Chapter 39   The Doctor is "In"

We had just finished the morning service at the orphanage in Haiti. I saw a boy who looked about 10 to 12 years old hobbling past. I asked the interpreter to stop the boy.

The boy had a cut at the top of his ankle, clear across the top of the foot. The interpreter asked the boy what had happened, and he replied that he got cut with a sugar cane leaf. When a sugar cane leaf dries up, it is very sharp. The infection made the cut look very bad.

We had an infirmary in one of the rooms where we had sent medical supplies. Things like band aids, gauze, Tylenol, rubbing alcohol, patches, different ointments and just general supplies were kept. We paid for a doctor to come out to the orphanage once a week. Many of the village people used his service.

I found a bottle of something. It said for cleansing cuts and wounds. I told the interpreter to tell the boy that this might really sting when I pour it on the wound. He said something and the boy just looked at me.

I told the interpreter to tell him that this will hurt. He said, "Yes, Yes. He knows."

I poured the stuff on the wound. It foamed a bit and the boy gritted his teeth like nothing happened. But it had to really smart!

We found some salve, gauze and bandage to wrap the ankle up. We added a prayer before he left and sent him on his way. I ask the interpreter to tell the boy to come back tomorrow and we will clean the wound. We had service that afternoon and again in the evening.

The next morning, we had service. I looked for the boy and he didn't even seem interested in coming back to the infirmary. I found the interpreter and had him get the boy. When he came in, we unwrapped the ankle to refresh the gauze. It was amazing how much better the cut looked. We poured the stuff on the wound to clean it, put on more of the goo, put on the gauze, wrapped the ankle with the bandage, added prayer, and sent him on his way. Praise God!

When I started to walk out the door, I couldn't get out. The people were lined up out the door and around the building. **The Doctor is "IN"!**

It made me realize that anything that we can do, it will help someone else. I wished that I had taken some basic Red Cross classes so I could have been able to help many of these people. We have so much opportunity in America. We should take every advantage to help others.

Jerry and I let the people in and listened to their needs. There were a lot of "headaches" and it became obvious that eating raw sugar cane is not good for the teeth. There were other cuts and scrapes that a little goo and prayer helped.

I am sure that there were no lawyers nearby to get me for malpractice. Because I was only practicing.

We are SO BLESSED to live in America.

Chapter 40   Bless Them

We were far up the coast of Haiti, north of the town of Gonaives (pronounced Go – ni – eve'). The actual region is called Three Rivers, but all we saw was a dried-up riverbed. We had passed a little village of maybe a couple of hundred of mud and grass huts. But rising high above these meager dwellings was this Church. Its steeple was at least 30 feet tall.

It was such a stark contrast to the poverty that was before you. I couldn't help but think that all this effort was to build a building to reach up to the sky rather than reaching out to the people. I'm sure that they do some outreach into the village, it just seemed so vain to have such an expensive Church amidst all this poverty.

We traveled on about another hour until we came to Anse-Rouge where we would be working from. They had a small block building that was divided into 3 rooms with doors connecting the rooms for us to stay in. The roof was tin with the rafters spaced about 5' apart. No doubt they didn't have to worry about the weight of snow on the roof.

It was nice in that we all had army cots to sleep on. Bro Tommy Ramsey and Bro Jerry Williams took the beds in the 3rd room. Jewel Williams (Jerry's wife), Sharleen Woodyard, Teresa Akers, Lucy French and Linda (my wife) took the middle room, and Robert Combs and myself took the front room. We all felt good about the idea that the women were safer in the middle.

The next morning, it was time to clean up, we walked up the road to where a well pump was located. It was a town gathering place because this was the only place where you could get fresh water. There were 2 young men that arrived that looked like they were in their late teens. Their job was to pump the well for all the community.

Once these 2 guys started pumping, they got a rhythm going that lasted nonstop for over half an hour. People were lined up with their containers to collect water for their home. Each person stepping up when they were next.

There are no "Rock Stars" or Superstars for kids to look up to. But when these two fellows began pumping water, you could see the look of the younger boys thinking, "Someday, I will grow up and be the one pumping the water".

When it came time for our ladies to wash their hair, the locals had the greatest time watching them wash and rinse their hair. The little children wanted to touch their long hair. Sharleen, Jewel, Teresa, Lucy and Linda had an impromptu "beauty parlor" that really bonded the townspeople to them. All the comforts of home.

Down the road, within walking distance, was a building that was built by Care International. Care is an organization that feeds people through donations. The building was a nice block building with steel rafters and tin roof. Care had used the building to store food for the people. After Baby Doc was ousted, the people broke the doors down and dispersed the food to the villagers.

We decided to use this building for a service. As the people that we were working with began the Church service, they introduced the two young men that broke into the building. The crowd cheered these men for getting the food out to the people.

When I say "crowd" that is the only way to describe it. It was dark, there was no electricity, and the only light that we had was a Coleman gas lantern that I held up as high as I could. The eyes of the people were all that you could see. We had no idea of the number of people that came to the service. All we can say is, the eyes of the people just disappeared off into the distance.

As Bro. Ramsey was preaching, people outside started throwing rocks at the building. The rocks were hitting the roof and made loud sounds as they hit the sheets of tin. The crowd began to get restless and frightened by the sounds. We could see that we were losing control of the situation.

We knew we needed to get out of the building before the people panicked and somebody got hurt. As we started towards the door, we grabbed the belt of the person in front of us to stay together. We formed this single line and worked our way out the building.

Chapter 41   **Show Them, Lord**

. . . . . thump, thump, thump, thump, thump, thump, thump. What is that sound?

I awake from a good sleep with this faint sound that I hear. It's getting gradually louder and louder. Where am I? What day is this? Let's see, this is Wednesday, so we are north of Gonaieve, Haiti. Now I remember!

There will be no light switch because there is no electricity. I think I left my flashlight right beside my sleeping cot. Sure enough, here it is. My watch says 2:00 am.

thump, thump, thump, thump, thump, thump, thump, thump, thump. What is that sound? It's closer!

We had service earlier that evening. They had stoned the building that we were trying to have service in.

Thump, thump, thump, thump, thump, thump, thump. What is that sound?

It was louder now as I realized that it was a large crowd of people coming down the road banging things together, chanting in step and in unison.

Thump, thump, thump, thump, thump, thump, thump.

It all stopped. It now got quiet.

The crowd was in front of our three-room building that we were staying in. It was the voodoo people trying to scare us away. We were going to change the lives of people by leading them to Jesus. The voodoo people did not want is in their area.

There was no way that we were going to let these people put fear on us.

2 Timothy 1:7 *For God hath not given us the spirit of fear; but of power, and of love, and of a sound mind.*

Our interpreter wasn't staying with us, so he couldn't do anything. I have the Baptism of the Holy Ghost and Speak in Tongues when I pray. So I thought I'd go outside and just Speak in Tongues. Maybe it would come out in Creole.

Act 2:4 *And they were all filled with the Holy Ghost, and began to speak with other tongues, as the Spirit gave them utterance.*
Act 2:6 *Now when this was noised abroad, the multitude came together, and were confounded, because that every man heard them* **speak in his own language.**

It was worth a try! I went to the door to go outside. It was locked! Our interpreter had the key! There was nothing we could do!

There was really nothing to worry about. The building was block with a tin roof. They couldn't afford oil to start a fire. Our wives were protected by being in the middle room.

But in my heart, I thought. Lord, you've got to show them that we are yours.

Send down lightening or something to show them that we are yours.

Well, in the other room, Bro Tommy and Bro Jerry were praying. They could hear the commotion going on out front. There was nothing they could do because the back door was lock, too.

Bro Tom told us latter that something told him to pray for rain. He told Jerry, so they began to pray.

Meanwhile, in the front room. Things weren't any better. They began to chant and make noise again to scare us.

What happened next just absolutely shocked us all.

It started to rain.

Little patters of rain. Hitting the tin. Not sounding like the rocks of hate that we heard earlier, but little patters of blessing in an area that hadn't had rain in months.

God was blessing them with rain!

The rain grew in intensity and the people outside were overjoyed with the rain.

I was wanting them to be struck with lightening.

God was wanting to bless them with rain.

The crowd dispersed and lost interest in us. They went home.

God 1 – voodoo 0

But wait, there is more.

The next day we had a Baptism down by the sea. We had over 80 people come to be Baptized in the Name of Jesus.

Gen 50:20 *But as for you, ye thought evil against me; but God meant it unto good, to bring to pass, as it is this day, to save much people alive.*

Chapter 42   Just a Kiss!

There are so many ways that you can be a blessing. There are so many times that the Lord wants to rebuke or reprove or instruct someone. The Lord wants us to be an example to those around us, of what it really means to be a Christian.

We were down in Brownstown, Jamaica. Brownstown is not a city or village where tourist would visit. It is a town that is pure Jamaica. The sights, sounds and smells remind you that you are in another world.

It is just a little town in the mountains, but for the locals, it is the market that brings them there. On Wednesdays, people from all over central Jamaica come to trade their goods. On the Tuesday night before, people arrive and find a place to set up their goods and also find a place to sleep among their goods. We would be driving back from a Church service late at night way back from the central part of Jamaica, and the city would be alive preparing for the "Market Day" on Wednesday.

Wednesday morning arrives with excitement as people from everywhere start arriving on the Tap taps, buses, cars, horse carts and back packs. As you wander through the market isles, you will find everything. A man standing calling out that he has fish and beside him is a 5-gallon plastic bucket filled with water and fish he caught that morning in the sea.

Next to him might be a row of potatoes or stalks of bananas and oranges spread out on the ground. Everyone is selling something that they caught, grew or made. There would be bags of beans or rice being sold just as soon as one would sell his fish. Trading and bartering were the normal.

Someone would have a wood carving that took hours to do. Then sanded, stained and polished to a beautiful finish. They might have a day's work in carving the figurine. Some of the carvings were worthless because of the artist lifestyle. For example, some of the figurines were of sexual nature, or smoking pipes for marijuana smokers. These items they were carving to try to get to the markets down on the coast were the tourist from the cruise ships would come to port.

But some of the items would be beautiful carvings of pictures, serving plates, bowls and decanters. These were very beautiful. A person would have a little shop that they would want you to step into that was no bigger than a closet. He or she would have all kinds of things on the walls, hanging from the ceiling and under a makeshift countertop that they would have for sale. It was a bad omen for a salesperson to lose the first sale of the day. So, going early in the morning put you as a buyer at an advantage.

In the 25 times that I went to Jamaica, I only bought a few things, but it was fun to be among the people in their own environment. Most of the people knew that you were missionaries having meetings in the different Churches. We had great respect for them, and they knew it.

Bargaining was the way of life. If you didn't bargain for a good price, you weren't respected. It showed that you didn't have value or respect of money. If you gave too much, it showed that you were frivolous with money. If a man came up to you with a vase and he asked for $100 dollars for it, you countered with $10. Of course, he would say, "Oh, that is not enough", and would ask for $50.00. You would say $15 and he would say $25 and you both would agree on $20. And $20 was a good price for him and not an insult. The sad part about the bargaining is that you know it would be sold for $150 in Pier One Imports in America.

There is a group of people in Jamaica called Rastafarians. (Ras – ta – far' – ions) They are the people that ushered in the "dread locks" hairstyle that you see people wear. Most of the Dreadlocks that you see in America are extensions, but these dread locks are hair has been growing for years and is matted and unkempt. The Rastafarians believed that Ganja (marijuana) is the "fruit of the Lord" and they would smoke it constantly. It is a part of their worship service. Raga

124

music that you hear in America is from this group. Bob Marley was one of their stars and spread their message when he was alive.

When Bob Marley died, they buried him in a place called 9 Mile, which was only about 20 miles from where we were staying at the time. I thought about going to the service. It would be a great place to do some "street witnessing" to the people that would attend. Nobody in our group wanted to go with me, it wouldn't be very smart to go alone, so I let it alone. It was a good thing that I didn't go, I found out later that over 7,000 people attended the funeral.

When we would have meetings in the Churches up in the mountains, you would smell the marijuana being smoked outside the Church. It is a weed, so it is plentiful and free. I would always want to be an example to those that were "bound up" with the habit of being high all the time that real joy comes from Jesus.

Linda and I were in Brownstown on market day. I saw a Rastafarian with a homemade "joint" of marijuana rolled up as big as a Cigar. Later that morning, I saw this same man lying in the gutter totally "wasted" on that joint.

This one morning, Linda and I got separated while in the market. That didn't bother me because Linda is a good Christian woman. She knows how to present herself to people and other women respected that.

I went into a shop that was selling different things. Now Rastafarians will not let you talk to them and they will not talk to you. In fact, they do not want you to even take a picture of them. Over on the side of the shop was this Rastafarian with his "queen". She was setting on a countertop and had a little finger sized music box. It was one of those little things that you would "plink" your fingers on or turn a little crank and it would play "pop goes the weasel" or something like that.

I knew that he wouldn't let me talk with them and he knew that I was a Christian Minister. But he wanted me to see that his "queen"

125

was making atmosphere music for him. He looked at me with this smug, "see what she does for me?"

Well, about that time, Linda comes in the shop, not knowing what was going on, came up to me and kissed me on the neck. I just looked at him and nodded "see what she thinks about me?"

I think it let a little "air out of his sails."

Later that day, I was walking through the marketplace. I saw a young man, about 18-20 years old, walking towards me. He was wearing a long trench coat that would have been much too warm to wear in this climate. He had a box of Colonel Sanders Fried Chicken in his hand.

As he approached me, he reached into the box of food and stuck his hand deep into the mashed potatoes and gravy. Nobody could see this, then he yelled out for all to hear. "Hey Preacher!" He then stuck his hand out for me to shake it. No one saw the gravy covered hand, but everyone saw that he was offering to me a friendly handshake. If I rejected the handshake, everyone would see it. People were watching not knowing what he was doing.

There just comes a place where you just have to stand your ground and just go where the chips fall.

I told him, "You wipe your hand and I will shake it."

He then put all his fingers in his mouth, sucked off the gravy, and then stuck his hand back out for me to shake it.

Well, whatever was going to happen next was going to happen. But no sooner than he extended his hand, people from all around grabbed the man and pulled him back. The crowd surrounded him and pulled him away. A number of people that had been in our services came up to me and apologized for his actions. They told me that he was not right in the head.

So, all is well that ends well.

Chapter 43   Some Remarkable People I have Met
Bro Harold Conway

The events that I have been sharing are not a reflection of the faith that I have in God, but in what God will do for His divine purpose. Here is the understanding that I believe is important.

I have watched ministries come and go, flourish for a season, and then break off into a group of people that is only "their" following. So many times, the ministry becomes to have a form of outreach, but only to build a personal following.

I met a Minister named Harold Conway from Tennessee. He had a nice Church with about 20-30 people attending the services. I meet him at a Ministers Convention at Bro. Carl Lewis' Church in Oak Hill WV.

Bro Conway was a quiet man. They would ask him to testify, I don't ever remember hearing him preach a service. But one night they turned the service over to him. I remember that he just set a chair in the altar and sat down. He asked for anyone that wanted prayer to come up to the front. The line went to the back of the Church.

Each and every person was prayed for or spoken to about their need. Bro. Conway took the time for each person. I believe that this part of the service went on for nearly an hour.

I remember that my great nephew went up for prayer. He was 14 or 15-years-old at the time. Bro Conway had never met my nephew, Tommy Akers, but he went on to tell Tommy that he was a young man that didn't care for football or baseball or any of the stuff out there in the world, but that Tommy liked to make music in the Church. He told him, "God was going to reward you and give you a guitar that no man can purchase."

After Church, Tommy wanted me to take him to music stores. He was really excited and wanted to buy this guitar. We searched and search and found nothing. I told Tommy that Bro Conway said, "no man can purchase."

So, this is the end of the story. But wait. About 7 months later, a member of a Church in upstate West Virginia, retired from the Gretsch Company that makes guitars. He decided to hand make a one-off guitar and give it to his Pastor. The Pastor thanked him even though he didn't know how to play a guitar.

We had invited this Pastor to our Church for a meeting. He didn't know anything about the prophesy that was given to Tommy. He happened to bring the guitar with him, and when he saw Tommy at our Church, he felt led of God to give him the guitar.

Bro. Conway said in the prayer, "God was going to reward him and give him a guitar that no man can purchase."

Chapter 44   H. Richard Hall

I've met many people who say they knew Bro. Hall. They have been in his services and they have been blessed by his Ministry. I met one man who said that he stayed in a motel room for hours and listened to Bro Hall preach on tapes. That didn't teach him what we knew by working with the man.

I know him in a different way. I was a part of the work in Cleveland Tennessee. I started just driving Bro. Hall to the services and I left 12 years later as the Presbyter of the Ministerial Association. I was there to be a part of building the first Church using shovels to dig out the basement. I later started the Printing Department in that basement.

We couldn't convince him to rent a tractor to dig out the basement, so we did it with shovels. I learned so much thru all those years. You couldn't buy that education. Bro Hall has one word to describe him. He was tenacious. The word that we made up to really describe what we learned from him was "stick-to-it-ism". We learned to get something done even if you didn't have the tools to work with, or the money to work with, or people standing with you to help. You just learn to have "stick-to-it-ism". I write this with tears of respect in my eyes.

He enjoyed life. One night we left Dallas, Tx after having services with Bro W.V. Grant. Bro. Hall was scheduled to be a tent service 1,100 miles away in Melborne, FL the next night. He and I would switch driving every couple of hours. It was in the north Florida panhandle area when I was driving in the wee hours before sunrise. I was rolling about 105 mph because we were in the section where it was nothing but pine trees growing for the paper mills. Nothing for miles and miles but trees. I was making great time, when Bro Hall woke up. He looked at the speedometer, looked at the trees hurling by, laid back down and then said, "Keep it under 90 mph". He slept the rest of the way.

I watched Bro Hall, take a bunch of guys like myself and give us a chance, and encourage us to do something for the Lord. None of us "inherited" a Church or followed the footsteps of our fathers in their ministries. We were from all walks of life with a sincere desire to do something for the Lord. Bro Hall gave us that chance. Many missionaries, teachers, Pastors, musicians and other Ministries came from our group.

We all learned to create something from nothing. "Fight a good fight." "Contend for the Faith." "Apply our heart to every work under the sun." If you fall or fail, get back up. You can't learn this in Bible College. You could only learn this through hard knocks. Dropping on your knees, get up and have "stick-to-it-ism".

There was a song that Bro Hall would sing, "All things are possible, only believe."

Chapter 45   Don Warren

Don Warren was just barely a teenager when he started to help a minister, named H. Richard Hall, put up gospel tents and play guitar in his services. One day Bro Hall told Don to get up to the organ and play it. That started a lifelong step of faith and devotion to the work of the Lord that Don Warren has fulfilled.

If you try to find Bro Don somewhere, the best place to start looking is wherever you find a Keyboard. After traveling millions of miles in tent revivals, Church Revivals and any other Church services, you will find Bro Don making music. If he stays at a friend's house and they have a piano, you will find Don quietly playing the piano with a cup of coffee and some bread.

Any organist in the Churches that I have been with, will always say, "I'd love to play like Don Warren."

Bro Don, James Rogers, myself and some other musicians, went to a recording studio just south of Louisville, Kentucky. There had been many "famous groups" that had used this recording studio, many names that you would know. Even "Tiny Tim" used this studio when he recorded "Tip toe, through the Tulips".

After hours of recording songs, we went to mix down the "tracts". This is the hardest part of a good recording. You listen to the songs and adjust the tones and volume levels to get the sound that you want. It takes longer to do the mixing, than it does to play the songs.

After 45 minutes of mixing the music, the engineer just folded his hands and went "silent" on us. He said, "What is a matter with you people?" Every group that comes in there wants their "tract" turned up. He said they always end up in arguments and fights. But you guys always ask for your tracts to be turned down so the other person can be heard.

If any scripture would describe Bro Don Warren, it is this.

1 Corinthians 4:1 *Let a man so account of us, as of the ministers of Christ, and stewards of the mysteries of God.*

1 Corinthians 4:2 *Moreover it is required in stewards, that a man be found faithful.*

As Bro H. Richard Hall passed on, Bro Don Warren continued on. His faithfulness in small things as a young man, has carried and strengthen him all the days of his life.

Luke 16:12 *And if ye have not been faithful in that which is another man's, who shall give you that which is your own?*

Chapter 46   Bro Tommy Ramsey

God Knows and God Cares

Bro Tommy Ramsey is a Pastor with a real heart for Mission work. He and Bro Pat Webb built several Churches in Haiti and Jamaica. But their work was much more than building Churches. Their desire was to feed and clothe people as they preached the Gospel.

Bro Tommy always sang and carried a guitar with him. One song that he loved to sing was "The Great Speckled Bird". In fact, the people enjoyed it so much that he became known as "Speckled Bird" in Jamaica. It would always bring a smile to each person when they would talk about him.

Bro Tommy had gone overseas for over 50 years. His heart was with the people. He didn't go for a crowd or to be seen. He just wanted to help the people.

But time marches on. It is hard on the body to do mission work. While the people of the countries are used to the hardships that they have to face daily, going on mission trips are quite a change from the comforts of home for the mission worker. You turn on a faucet to shave in the morning but instead, you find a pale of rainwater to shave and cleanup on the mission field. Everything is different. In America, we take everything for granted.

Bro Tommy was now on his 50th trip overseas. He was now 80 years old. He was considering this to be his last. But how do you stop going when you have been doing this for years. It isn't as easy to do what you have to do when your body is now older. Traveling those mountain roads becomes less safe. Sleeping on a cot isn't as easy when your 80 years old as it was when you were in your 30's.

And what does God think about this.

So, we were in a little Church in the mountains of Jamaica. It was the last service of the week. It was the last service of the mission trip. And Bro. Tommy knew this would be the last mission trip that he would go on. His 50th mission trip.

As Bro. Tommy stepped up to the pulpit to preach, a little bird flew into the Church and landed on the Bible stand. There were no windows in the Church. There was only a string of lights to light up the Church. But this little bird landed on the Bible Stand and turned its' head to look at Bro Tommy.

Did this little speckled bird come to listen one more time to the "speckled bird"?

It was as if the Lord himself knew that this was the last service and he sent the little bird into the Church to say, *"Well done thou good and faithful servant."*

Chapter 47   **Bishop Earl Chavis**

Some people think that being the bishop is a title that is given to you because you have pastored or been in the service of the Lord for a long time.   But a true Bishop is a person that Churches and their people look up to and he is always there for them.

I met Bishop Chavis over 20 years ago and he fulfils the Bible definition of a Bishop. Having been with the Bishop in service in four states, it is obvious that Pastors and Ministers esteem him highly. That respect comes not from a vote from some committee, but the respect and confidence from people.

1st Timothy 3:1-7 *This is a true saying, If a man desire the office of a bishop, he desireth a good work.*
A bishop then must be blameless, the husband of one wife, vigilant, sober, of good behaviour, given to hospitality, apt to teach;
Not *given to wine, no striker, not greedy of filthy lucre; but patient, not a brawler, not covetous;*
One *that ruleth well his own house, having his children in subjection with all gravity;*
(For if a man know not how to rule his own house, how shall he take care of the church of God?)
Not *a novice, lest being lifted up with pride he fall into the condemnation of the devil.*
Moreover *he must have a good report of them which are without; lest he fall into reproach and the snare of the devil.*

Bishop Chavis has been there and helped many Churches across the Nation. He has ministered to Eskimos in Alaska, to Indians at their reservation in Oklahoma, and countless Churches across the country. Whatever the need, he has been a listening ear and prayerful ear to keep the work of the Lord strong.

Chapter 48   **Brother Timothy Spell**

Evangelist

2nd Timothy 4:5 But *watch thou in all things, endure afflictions, do the work of an evangelist, make full proof of thy ministry.*

The work of an Evangelist is work indeed. To many people, they feel that it is all about being a good entertainer. But Churches today are on the fine line of wanting to be entertained, rather than be fed the "Word of God."

For the last 20 years that I have been in services with Bro Spell, I have heard the finest of Biblical messages, the most professional singing, and all delivered by person with a wonderful personality. He has been a blessing to my soul.

I was attending a Church conference in North Carolina. I had never been to this convention before and knew no one there. But low and behold, there was Bro Spell. After service, he made the effort to take me around and introduce me to almost every Minister who was there. Now, I mean he introduced them to me by their first name. This was not just an exhibition of memorization; these were friends of his. Each and every one of these men seemed to be close friends of his.

This is when I saw that they really were friends of his. He wasn't just some entertainer that performed, and then went over into a corner because he thought that he was some superstar that wasn't to be bothered. Bro Spell fulfilled from his heart the scripture,

Proverbs 18:24 A *man that hath friends must shew himself friendly: and there is a friend that sticketh closer than a brother.*

What a wonderful example to show.

1 Thessalonians 2:8 So *being affectionately desirous of you, we were willing to have imparted unto you, not the gospel of God only, but also our own souls, because ye were dear unto us.*

Chapter 49   Everything has a time and a season.

Ecc 3:1 *To every thing there is a season, and a time to every purpose under the heaven:*

The events in this book happened over a period of years. I could write of more, but it would only sound like I am trying to boast of some great calling in my life.

This book is about you fulfilling your calling in life. I have no doubt that you have experienced situations just as miraculous as what I have written about and yet you haven't shared them with others.

John 12:32 *And I, if I be lifted up from the earth, will draw all men unto me.*

Every time you share some event that you believe that God is in, you are lifting up Jesus. You don't know what an impact it will do to someone else's life. There are so many Churches today that will not allow you to even testify about something that the Lord has done for you.

Even if the problems that you are facing are not working out the way that you hoped they would, you might feel like a failure. But keep in mind that God's word is always true.

Romans 8:28 *And we know that all things work together for good to them that love God, to them who are the called according to his purpose.*

You can't wait for a "better day" to share the Lord to anyone, because the trial or battle that you are going through, is so you can learn something from God. The best way to overcome the problem is look at the solution.

Hebrews12:2 *Looking unto Jesus the author and finisher of our faith; who for the joy that was set before him endured the cross, despising the shame, and is set down at the right hand of the throne of God.*

You may feel that you don't know enough Bible, or you aren't religious enough to share "the Lord" with anyone else. But that is the point. It is not your religion that leads a person to Jesus, it is your relationship with Him.

Acts 4:13 *Now when they saw the boldness of Peter and John, and perceived that they were unlearned and ignorant men, they marveled; and they took knowledge of them, that they had been with Jesus.*

Do you notice how that hardly anyone talks to each other anymore? They are texting someone else or checking to see if anyone else is trying to text them. We are all looking for acceptance from someone. We all look to see if we have any "Likes". In fact, we desire to be liked so much that even our conversations are filled with "likes". Like every sentence that, like, you hear. Like, they use the word "like" so many times. Like, I can't even hear, like, what they are, like, saying.

Philippians 3:13-15 *Brethren, I count not myself to have apprehended: but this one thing I do, forgetting those things which are behind, and reaching forth unto those things which are before,*
I press toward the mark for the prize of the high calling of God in Christ Jesus.
Let us therefore, as many as be perfect, be thus minded: and if in any thing ye be otherwise minded, God shall reveal even this unto you.

We are in a time where everyone says that it doesn't matter what you do because God understands. No, that is just religion. It does matter.

Any lifestyle that you do is ok, God is forgiving. No, that is just religion. It does matter.

When you are in a relationship walk with the Lord, it matters **to you** if you please him.

Hebrews 10:22-25 *Let us draw near with a true heart in full assurance of faith, having our hearts sprinkled from an evil conscience, and our bodies washed with pure water.*
Let us hold fast the profession of our faith without wavering; (for he is faithful that promised;)
And let us consider one another to provoke unto love and to good works:
Not forsaking the assembling of ourselves together, as the manner of some is; but exhorting one another: and so much the more, as ye see the day approaching.

God's will for you is to live a pure and holy life before Him.

Romans 12:1 *I beseech you therefore, brethren, by the mercies of God, that ye present your bodies a living sacrifice, holy, acceptable unto God, which is your reasonable service.*

He doesn't force you to do His will, but His will is the best for you.

Romans 12:2 *And be not conformed to this world: but be ye transformed by the renewing of your mind, that ye may prove what is that **good**, and **acceptable**, and **perfect**, will of God.*

Your walk with God should be different. Not conformed to this world and its' fashions. Don't conform your choices to the way the world makes choices. That is religion.

The scripture in Romans shows how we can grow in God's will.

Romans 12:1 *that **ye** may prove what is that **good, and acceptable, and perfect** will of God.*

Do you want a ***good*** walk with the Lord?

Or do you want an ***acceptable*** walk with the Lord?

Or do you want the ***perfect*** will of God?

See, it is your choice.

To have that perfect will of God is to do, "*not my will, but Thy will be done.*"

The Bible clearly states what will happen in the last days.

2nd Timothy 3:1-5 *This know also, that in the last days perilous times shall come.*
For men shall be lovers of their own selves, covetous, boasters, proud, blasphemers, disobedient to parents, unthankful, unholy,
Without natural affection, trucebreakers, false accusers, incontinent, fierce, despisers of those that are good,
Traitors, heady, highminded, lovers of pleasures more than lovers of God;
*Having a **form of godliness**, but denying the power thereof: from such turn away.*

You will have to make a difference! You will have to reach for a relationship with Jesus. The world will just want religion. "*Having a **form of godliness***", but you will have a personal relationship with the Lord.

I refer to a man mentioned in the Old Testament named Enoch. He knew God, he walked with God.

Genesis 5:24 *And Enoch walked with God: and he was not; for God took him.*

He walked with God.

Not beside Him.

Not near Him.

But with Him.

Matthew 19:26 *But Jesus beheld them, and said unto them, With men this is impossible; but with God all things are possible.*

It's now your call.

It's your calling.

Walk with God.

Have a personal relationship with Jesus.

Chapter 50   Your Turn

I have no doubt in my heart that, as you read this book, there have been things that have happen to you in your lifetime, that was just as miraculous as what you read in this book. Well, here is my request to you.

Write up an experience that the Lord did in your life. I would love to put it in a chapter of the next book so email it to me.

I am serious, I want to put together a book that tells the story of what the Lord has done in other people's life. I want you to be a part of that. We have to pass this on.

Joel 1:3 *Tell ye your children of it, and let your children tell their children, and their children another generation.*

I want you to email this to me. I will put it together and get it published. This is your chance.

My email address is: BroCraigStrain@gmail.com

Share what the Lord has done for you.   It will bless others.

Watch for the book in the summer 2020!